RE-THINKING BIBLICAL STORY AND MYTH

Critical Essays on Biblical Interpretation

ARNOLD M. ROTHSTEIN

Selected Lectures at the
Theodor Herzl Institute
1986-1995

University Press of America, Inc.
Lanham • New York • Oxford

Copyright © 1998
University Press of America,® Inc.
4720 Boston Way
Lanham, Maryland 20706

12 Hid's Copse Rd.
Cummor Hill, Oxford OX2 9JJ

Library of Congress Cataloging-in-Publication Data

Rothstein, Arnold M.
Re-thinking biblical story and myth : selected lectures at the
Theodore Herzl Institute / Arnold M. Rothstein.
p.   cm.
1. Bible. O.T.–Criticism, interpretation, etc. I. Title.
BS1192.R627 1998   221.6—dc21   98-7749 CIP

ISBN 0-7618-1166-4 (cloth: alk. ppr.)
ISBN 0-7618-1167-2 (pbk: alk. ppr.)

In Gratitude To My Wife

CONTENTS

Foreword

This book is composed of selected lectures delivered over the course of a ten-year association with the Theodor Herzl Institute in New York City. The framework of study was non-doctrinal, involving critical analysis of the vocabulary and thought contained in biblical story and myth, from historical, philosophical, and sociological perspectives.

A weekly lecture series was delivered over the course of twenty-six sessions a year, under the following titles:

1986: The Origins of Hebrew Monotheism
1987: The Jesus of History
1988: The Jews as a Pariah People:
      Examination of the Weberian Thesis
1989-
1990: Folklore in the Bible
1991 Invalidation and Intolerance in the Founding and
      Development of New Religions: Christianity and Islam
1992: Theory of the Lost Tribes and Historical Understandings
1993: Political Factionalism in the History of Israel
1994: The Messiah Idea: Pretense and Imagery

The author extends his thanks to the Theodor Herzl Institute for its confidence, encouragement, and endorsement, as well as for the privilege of studying with its members in a congenial and edifying atmosphere. The educational policy of the Institute has always been defined by the goal of advancement of knowledge towards broadened perspectives and greater self-understanding.

◆

Regarding Content

An historical impulse occurs within us as a natural tendency even when not intended. We ask: when did an event take place? How did it happen? What produced it? The questions become inappropriate when the material under consideration has to do with moral instruction, e.g., the story of Cain and Abel as a bulwark against wanton murder, for the usual accompaniment to such asking is the tendency to anachronization and retrojection; i.e., the application of, latter-day understandings and judgments to a mode of thought and vocabulary culturally distant in time and place.

It has to be emphasized that a myth is not — as some think — an error; it encases a truth apprehended through poetic and impressionist involvement. However, frequently, it is the encasement of the myth that is euhemerized or converted into historical occurrence. The individual becomes involved in the story personally and "experiences it" – as it were. The story of the paradisial garden of Eden is one example; as etiological or explanatory myth, it becomes transformed into an unspecificable — yet historicized — occurrence. Thus, the various lectures contained within this book are connected by a particular perspective. They call for an analytic orientation towards biblical modes of thought; i.e., an understanding that biblical writing is pointed towards moral teaching, theodicy, and polemic, and not towards historiography. It is hoped that such understanding will guide the reader through the various selections.

Regarding Matters of Style and Presentation

Some people are unable even to pronounce words in another language because of an internalized conviction that their native tongue is superior to — or, at least, suffices for — any other possible mode of expression. Yet, unconscious or blithe ethnocentrism is not a justification for persistence in habitual Anglicization of *all* non-English locutions. To sound out "Elijah" as *Ee-lye-juh*, is not only a mere distortion of the tonality of Hebrew pronunciation; the *juh* sound obscures and destroys the vocalization *Yahu* or *Yah*, the God-appellative woven into the very name of Eliyahu (*E-lee-yah-hoo*) itself. * Whether it is the result of chauvinist feeling or the bad habits justified by it, the practice need not be abetted unto perpetuity. Accordingly,

*Names such as Eliyahu, Yishayahu, Yirmiyahu, Yoshi-yahu, Ḥizki-yahu are known as theophorus; i.e., they contain the name of the deity itself – yahu or yah.

transliterations of Hebrew pronunciation of Hebrew words are presented in preference to their Anglicized versions. Yet, some compromises are inevitable, Thus, where there is reference to a biblical *book*, the Anglicized version of the title is maintained, while the name of the person is transliterated in its Hebraic form; thus, "Yeḥezkel exclaims in Ezekiel 23:6...". The result of the compromise is an inevitable cumbersomeness which, it is hoped, will not prove too distracting.

Frequently, both Hebrew and English versions of a name will be given, as in Yaacov (Jacob) or Kurush (Cyrus), or a double spelling will be used (Nebuchadrezzar/Nebuchadnezzar) because that is the way the name appears in the Hebrew text, the N and R sounds being indeterminate. With regard to place names, *Kenaan* is closer to an original Semitic pronunciation than is the distortion, "Kaynan," and *Mitzrayim* is a much earlier name than Egypt, its cognates being found on ancient inscriptions. The name Moses is preserved as is, because it is probably closer to the original Egyptian sounds – (*meses*, meaning begotten) – than the Hebrew version would be. The ḥ (kh) sound has no English equivalent. While close to the aspirant h, it is closed-throated, somewhat similar to the sound emitted when snoring in exhalation.

The term Yahu-ism (referring to the period of the eleventh-sixth century BCE) is employed, as distinct from "Judaism," in point of philosophical development. Yahu-ism represents the divine name in Israelite history in what later comes to be labelled the "theology" of ancient Israel; one cannot, therefore, properly refer to "Judaism," the mature product of later centuries of development, without anachronization. The use of the term "The Lord," as a translation of YHWH or Yahu, is rejected as inadequate.

Each lecture is a self-contained unit and one may read the presentations in any order, although Lecture 1 may serve as a general introduction. It is recommended that references to biblical texts – given in the Notes or in the body itself – be consulted so that context and nuance become clearer. Although one gets a general idea of the content through the digest presented within the body of the lecture, invariably something is either lost or omitted. There probably is some general familiarity with the basic content of Lectures 1, 2 and 3, however, Lectures 4, 5 and 6 contain material that is not readily at hand through informal acqaintance. It is here that references to original texts should be consulted.

RE-THINKING
BIBLICAL
STORY
AND
MYTH

1. Variety of Folklore in the Bible

Some diverse Biblical incidents are presented which reveal the variety of ways in which a message is portrayed in folklore. Actually, variety *within* folklore is a dominant characteristic *of* folklore so that one is saying much the same thing when speaking of folklore and variety. It suffices to say that the variety of folklore is the material of which the drama of the Bible is constructed.

Introduction

The examining of folklore helps us to recover an ancient way of thinking and understanding, a way involving imagery and not definitions. As Ernst Cassirer tells us, it gives us the non-intellectual or affective side of the mind, and helps us to see significance. Detached analysis prevents sympathetic involvement and, as such analysis proceeds, myth gets replaced by philosophy and science, even as ritual gets expressed in art.

Mythic modes of expression resolve into metaphors, in which the ancient belief evaporates, and merely a verbal shell remains. For instance, disease and bodily affliction were, in the language of the times, "the assault of demons." We still have a verbal shell as a reminder of the older belief: a heart *attack* [by whom?] or a heart *seizure* [again, by whom?]

Matters of common belief and understanding were expressed within myth: man's soul takes flight at his demise, strength resides in one's hair, leprosy is punishment for impiety; misconduct on the part of a king, such as David or Ahab, can produce drought. It was a commonplace thought that forces of nature are influenced by human behavior, much like the commonplace thought that, we, today, entertain: the planetary sign of the zodiac under which we are born determines our character.

Thoughts which we express today in rational terms were presented in impressionist images. Even ideas came to be represented as beings or persons! Such ideas were not apprehended by conceptual operations, but through direct relationship to a live being. Thus, personification as a method of articulation, was well-nigh universal: *God led Israel out of Mitzrayim with a strong hand and an outstretched arm.* His *voice* is thunder and his *breath* is the wind. This excerpt from Psalm 29, indeed the entire psalm, is replete with this kind of personification. In other words, the personification of ideas, imagery, and the language of marvels are basic techniques of articulation and explanation, myth being the natural language of religion.

Magic as a Force

A dominant feature of an ancient world-view was the belief in magic as a pervasive force in the universe. There was no neutrality in the universe, but only good and bad magic; the good could be produced by special formulae and skilled practitioners, while the bad had to be cordoned off and guarded against. An example of the latter and its pervasiveness is found in the tabu against looking back.

Aeskylos and Sophokles tell us that, in propitiatory rites to the Furies, the performer was not to turn around. In the epic tales that were told of Greek heroes, Aeneas - in departing from burning Troy in the 13th century BCE - could not look back, and the famous Orpheus had to lead Eurydike out of Hades without turning around. The common rule was to avoid head-turning (which could be seen as a sign of regret), lest bad magic be diffused and distributed. In the biblical narrative concerning the destruction of Sedom (Genesis 19: 17,26) this tabu was broken, with dire consequences. What happened to Lot's wife (who turned into salt-stone) would serve as a warning to others who would break the tabu.

In marked contrast - but still in evidence of the pervasiveness of magic as a universal force - one reads in Genesis 30:11 of Zilpah, Leah's handmaiden, who bears Yaacov (Jacob) a son, and Leah declares: *BaGad* (also referred to as *Begad!* and even *Egad*(s)!) The usual and somewhat insipid translation tells us that "Fortune [Gad] has come." Our understanding is sharpened when we learn that Gad was a Kenaanite deity of luck and that this child of Zilpah's was named for that deity. The site of a shrine to the cult of the god, Gad, was actually called Baal-Gad, located in the valley of Lebanon under Mount Hermon, and is referred to in three places in the Book of Joshua, 11:17, 12:7 and 13:5; one additional site was at Migdal-Gad, near Ashkelon (Joshua, 15:37). Two of the spies sent by Moses in the desert to bring back information about the land of Kenaan bore the name of this deity: Gaddi-el, son of Sodi, from the tribe of Zevulun (Numbers 13:10), and Gaddi, son of Sussi, from the tribe of Manasseh (Number 13:11). It also was the personal name of one of the kings of Israel in the 8th century BCE: Menahem, son of Gaddi (2 Kings, 15:14, 17).

The name, of course, means luck or Fortune, and to invoke the name of a deity was thought to be equivalent to receiving the divine essence, through diffusion of the force of magic. (Later material will deal with contact with holiness through clothing and fetishes.) Luck was popular among the Romans as the goddess Fortuna, and also as Tyche (chance). By the time of the prophet Yisha-yahu (Isaiah) in mid-8th century BCE, the worship of Gad was full-blown. The "Couch of Gad," referred to a table of dainties and sweet-meats, and was condemned roundly by the prophet: "But you who forsake YHWH... who prepare a table for Gad [Destiny or Fortune], and offer wine to Meni [goddess of Destiny who assigned fates], I will destine you to the sword..." (Isaiah 65:11-12). The vestige of offerings to Gad is found in the folk-pratice of "leavings" or *shir'ayim.* Well into the 19th century CE, it was considered proper not to consume every particle and crumb of food. These "leavings" were popular offerings to Fortune.

In addition to special formulae to evoke good magic, there were even natural substances that had the power to produce good magic. The following excerpt from Genesis 30:1, 14-17 reveals the setting in which the natural substance was to be employed:

"And when Raḥel saw that she bore Yaacov no children, Raḥel envied her sister; and said to Yaacov, Give me children, or else I die... And Reuven went in the days of wheat harvest, and found mandrakes in the field, and brought them to his mother Leah. Then Raḥel said to Leah, Give me, I pray you, of your son's mandrakes. And she said to her, is it a small matter that you have taken away my husband? and would you take away my son's mandrakes also. And Raḥel said, Therefore he shall lie with you tonight for your son's mandrakes."

Mandrakes - known also as love herbs - are called in Hebrew *Dudaim, Dud*_meaning to love. (The name Dvd (David) can also be vocalized as Dud.) Mandrakes, like the ginseng root, resemble the human form and because of the resemblance, are credited with magical powers. (The Arabs refer to the *Dud* as the "apple of the Jinns," the Jinn representing a fantastic being with unusual powers.) In Korea, the ginseng root is enormously popular and appears in a variety of potions. In *The Wars of the Jews,* Book vii, 6,3, the first-century historian, Josephus, tells us something of a magical, natural substance. He records the popular notion of the *Baaras Root* as protective against bad magic. When brought to sick persons, it drive away demons, "which are no other than the spirits of the wicked which enter into men that are alive and kill them, unless they can obtain some help against them." He recommends tying a dog to the plant, and when the animal wants to wander away, he plucks up the root and dies; *then* the root can be handled safely. (Note that the same object that is protective against unseen forces cannot be handled without safeguards.)

From the excerpt in Genesis, it is clear that the love herbs or man-drakes were used as aphrodisiacs and as an antidote against barrenness (which is why Raḥel sought them so eagerly). This use may also be seen in the reference to Aphrodite, who was sometimes referred to as "Our Lady of the Mandrake." In the Song of Songs, 7:14, the maiden tells her lover that she has stored for him mandrakes: "The love plants yield their fragrance." In English literature, one notes the poetic reference to the "love apple." A fur-ther example, revealing the diffusion of the idea of the power in natural sub-stances, was the custom in German folk medicine, of placing mandrakes un-der a bridal bed, presumably on the theory that proximity alone would be efficacious.

The prefatory comment regarding variety *within* folklore is recalled here. It is well understood that in language, there are many ways of saying the same thing; similarly, within folklore, a different customary practice poses no real problem of reconciliation; the detail is less important than the under-lying idea [of magic], and is actually a case of "the more the merrier." In other words, rather than seeing *variety* as contradiction, it is the actual es-sence of lore. Thus, to focus on the difficulty of tying a dog to the *Baaras Root* - rather than to uproot the plant oneself - can entangle one in a web which then obscures the underlying idea, i.e., that magic (good and bad) is a force in the universe. It has the power to produce good effects, if employed by a skillful practitioner.

The Heart as Centerpiece

If one would recover an ancient way of thinking and understanding, the role and force of magic must be recognized. Almost as important is the nomenclature of a specialized vocabulary, such as the place of the heart. The heart symbolized the total self; indeed, in sleep, the heart was said to depart from one.

Not only was the heart considered the seat of emotions, as in Exodus 7:14, (Paro's heart is stubborn), it was also the point of origin of mental processes. To "say in the heart" meant to think. Thus, in Genesis 17:17, regarding the birth of Yitzhak, Avraham 'said in his heart,' "Shall a child be born to him who is a hundred years old?" Or, as Genesis 27:41 recounts: "And Esau said in his heart...I will slay my brother." To think a thought was expressed as speaking to oneself - a rather rich metaphor!

To "steal the heart" meant to gain control over another person. In the "Land of the Dead," the gods of Mitzrayim weighed a person's heart on a scale (against a feather) as a test of total moral worth, while in the Egyptian *Book of the Dead* (Chapters 26-30), demons are referred to as "stealers of the heart," who robbed the dead of their consciousness. The seeming conflict between being dead and conscious at the same time is wonderfully revealing of a time-connected cultural difference. As mentioned earlier, to focus on what is considered a twentieth century contradiction creates an impediment to comprehending the thought processes of the twentieth century *prior* to the Common Era.

Stealing the heart as a manifestation of control is well-illustrated in the passage in Genesis 31:20: "And Yaacov outwitted Lavan" (literally, stole his heart), while in verse 26, Lavan complains: "what have you done that you have outwitted me?" (literally, stolen my heart). One may note that in its specialized vocabulary and nomenclature, the Bible expresses itself in the world - outlook of the day in which it, itself, is situated; thus, it reflects, in large part, the spirit of the age.

The Place of Marvels in Folklore

In this brief sampling of variety of folklore in the Bible, a chronological leap is now made to the Ninth Century BCE, to the period of Eli-yahu and Elisha, two charismatic holy men. In its richness, this period reveals much about the nature of folklore, in the process, telling us much about ourselves and our needs. Somewhat mysteriously, folk memories are preservative of some abiding internal need. In northern Israel, a folk-memory of marvellous deeds by holy men - who were able to exert their will on natural phenomena - was retained over centuries. This memory consisted of a rich abundance of marvel tales which were later incorporated into early Christianity, and remained as central and paramount to it.

First off, the very name which each of these men bears is highly suggestive and pregnant with significance: *Eli-Yahu* (or Eli-Yah) may represent a syncretism of two names for God: *El* and *Yahu* (or Yah). Literally, the conjoining declares that Yah[u] is [my] God. Similarly, *Elisha* involves the combining of two ideas: *El* and *Yisha* (or *El Yesha*), God will save or El [God] is my salvation. The elision of the *y* sound when *Elisha* is pronounced as one word, may be a result of rapid articulation; yet, the pronounciation itself expresses a syncretism in the concept of God, i.e., God is the source of salvation.

Next, it must be noted that the two books of *Kings,* in which the exploits of Eliyahu and Elisha are recorded, are not very good historical writing. There is little order and chronology, a tendency to break off a story and start another (suggesting different narrators), leading to questions of coherence and cogency. In some of the tales, one identifies the main character as Eliyahu; a variant of the story later appears in which the main character is Elisha. It is clear that in the process of retelling of a tale, discrepancy is bound to occur. Nevertheless, four major themes bearing on the nature of folklore may be identified: transposition of the personality through the operation of the force of magic, the exercise of will on natural phenomena, the archetype of the holy man solidified (a wonder-worker by speech and touch), holiness augments (or restores) life. In the presentation that follows there is an attempt to illustrate these discretely, yet there is surely overlap between them.

1. Transposition of the Personality Through the Operation of Magic [On Clothing]:

In 2 Kings 2:14, Elisha is seen putting on Eliyahu's mantle immediately after Eliyahu had disappeared in a whirlwind (v.11). Elisha, the disciple, now repeats the *exact same* marvel that Eliyahu had performed, namely, the parting of the waters of the river Yarden (Jordan). (Verse 8). In Verse 15, witnesses proclaim that now the spirit of Eliyahu rested on his disciple, Elisha. What is the significance of this mantle affair?

Some of us may recall the story of the Sorcerer's Apprentice in which the apprentice put on his master's costume and – in performing sorcery – produced a crisis (a flood). (Incidentally, the origin of the tale seems to have revolved around the Golem of Prague, a fantastic robot-like creature of the 16th Century, who would not stop fetching buckets of water). In another example of the power believed to reside in clothing, one may recall the story of "The Robe," presumably the garment recovered at the execution of a Jesus, which had magical powers. Similar powers were ascribed to the burial "Shroud of Turin" in which the body of a Jesus was believed to have been wrapped.

The link between personality and clothing may actually be seen in its rejection, the removal of clothing implying loss of identity or abasement. Some cults even require nakedness in the presence of the divine (or the shaving of the hair). Penitents often changed garments to extreme simplicity or even to rags as did the penitents of medieval Christendom or the acolytes of Buddhism. We may note how we picture the garb of a prophet in our minds: characteristically, it is the haircloth of humility, mentioned by the prophet Zechariah (13:4), as the garment worn "to deceive!"

At the other end of the scale, when it came to regal clothing, the traditional robes and crowns of royalty, some tabus were apparent. For instance, the crown of Good King Wenceslaus (of the famous Christmas carol by that name) could be worn only by the kings of Bohemia. In the period of the Nazi occupation, the Reichsprotektor, Reinhard Heydrich, violated the ban and put the crown on his head. (One notes that he was later assassinated.) Similarly, the clothes of the Mikado were bound up with his divine self so that it was fatal for anyone to wear them.

While some of us smile patronizingly at these thoughts, we still harbor some belief in a manifestation of the magic operating in the universe: the transposition of the personality *through* the clothing itself. It appears to be a case of liking one's own magic while rejecting the magic of others. Consider the New York Yankees baseball team of the Gehrig-DiMaggio days. It was said that it was the Yankee uniform that turned a mediocre performer–acquired from another team – into an outstanding player! Or consider the fetishist craze in which a delirious crowd will snatch pieces of clothing from a culture hero such as a famous football player. The open desirability of such "souvenirs" reveal how hard it is to eradicate the notion of magic in clothing.

2. The Exercise of Will on Natural Phenomena:

The language of the Bible expresses the world-outlook in which it itself is situated, i.e., the language of marvel. To the faithful, marvel is simply descriptive rather than unusual. In 2 Kings 6:5-7, an axe falls in the water from tree-chopping. Elisha throws in a stick and the axe floats to the surface. In the words of the text, "he [merely] made the iron to swim." This same story from the Ninth Pre-Century, was told of St. Benedict (480-543 C.E.) at Monte Cassino more than a millenium later.

In the following illustration, it can be seen that lore is repeated tale from generation to generation, persisting as explanation or theory. In 2 Kings 4:1-7, we read of a widow who is blessed by the prophet, Elisha, with an inexhaustible cruse of oil. Earlier, in 1 Kings 17:14-16, the tale is told of Elisha's mentor, Eliyahu, and the widow of Tzorfata (near Sidon, Lebanon), where a jar of meal is not spent, nor did the cruse of oil fail. The message in both cases (if they are indeed separate tales), seems to be that hospitality to itinerant saints brings the reward of an increase in food. (The theme that "generosity begets increase" is found repeatedly in Jewish tales.) Now, to ask about actuality of the event or its internal consistency, (did it occur with Eliyahu or with Elisha?), is to miss the point.

Embellishment does not undermine the explanatory power of the tale; on the contrary, it enhances it! That a holy man can affect natural phenomena is simply a self-evident world-view, similar to the accepted notion of many today, that the stars affect our destiny. To the faithful, who are concerned with astral effects on their lives, there is nothing unusual about such a commonplace.

Another example of the embedding and persistence of lore is found in the tale of 2 Kings 4:42-44. In a variant on the theme of the inexhaustible jar of meal, Elisha feeds 100 men with 20 loaves of barley and corn. An embellished variation of the story appears nine centuries later in *The Gospel According to Mark* 6:38-44: Five loaves of bread and two fish feed 5000 men.

3. The Archetype of the Holy Man Solidified

If one examines the careers of Eliyahu and Elisha closely, a pattern begins to emerge: wonder-working by speech and touch becomes a tradition in northern Israel, the home of charismatic holy men. This unsophisticated milieu produced several hasidic, holy-men types, among whom are found Honi the Circle-Drawer, and Hanina ben Dosa, the famed healer and wonder-worker. The success of such holy men lay in their meeting the simple needs of the country-side dwellers and in their resemblance to the folk-memory of Eliyahu and Elisha, the archetypal holy men.

The folk-memory of Eliyahu may be noted. He appears with remarkable suddenness in 1 Kings 17:1ff; absolutely nothing is related of his early life except that he is a Gileadite from the village of Tishbi, probably a rustic area north of the Yabbok River. Nine centuries later another holy man type is said to appear suddenly. In keeping with the folk-memory of Eliyahu, nothing is known of *his* early life. In the earliest gospel, that according to Mark (1:9), a Jesus simply appears at age 30 to take up his ministry. Indeed, the picture of a Jesus in gospel writing adheres to the Galilean Hasid-type of holy man. Moreover, the connection to Eliyahu is made explicit in the following gospel writings: Mark, 6:15, 8:28; Matthew 6:14; and Luke 9:18, 19. In response to the question ascribed to Jesus: "Whom do people say I am?" the answer was: "He is Elias [Eliyahu]."

4. Holiness Augments (or Restores) Life

In addition to persistence of thematic material and to its variation and expansion, one may also note thematic extension. For instance, that death itself can be overcome by holiness. "Death, where is your victory? Death, where is your sting?" (1 Corinthians 15:55) This is the claim of Pauline Christianity, and this idea of overcoming death has its matrix and incubation in northern Israel.

In 1 Kings 17:17-24, there is an account of Eliyahu reviving a widow's dead son. Eliyahu had been staying at the widow's house where she provided lodging and food for him. The widow reproaches Eliyahu for lodging with her and reminding God of her sins. The idea seems strange, yet the widow believed that by his holy presence and saintly life, her failings were, thereby, more starkly revealed; consequently, she was punished by the death of her son. Eliyahu revives her son to the woman's great joy. The marvel of reviving the dead had been demonstrated!

In 2 Kings 4:18-38, we see a variation of this tale, only this time, Elisha is the main character. Elisha receives lodging from a married couple in Shunem, who are childless. As a reward for her good deeds, Elisha promises the woman a son and she is blessed with a child. When he is already grown he dies, and the woman reproaches Elisha for deceiving her with the promise of a child. Elisha revives the son and returns him to his grateful mother. Again, the marvel of reviving the dead had been demonstrated!

Approximately nine centuries later a story is recorded in *The Gospel According to Luke* (7:11-17). The geographical venue is the same general area. There is a widow in the village of Nayin (Nain) near the town of Capharnaḥum, who has just lost a son who is being carried out of the town for burial. A holy man [a Jesus] approaches the bier, touches it, and tells the young man to arise, and he sits up alive. The teaching is clear: Death [i.e., sin] can be overcome by holiness. "Death, where is your victory? Death, where is your sting?" asks Paul. In this instance, the holy man can affect natural phenomena in extraordinary fashion! One can marvel at the staying power of a story; variation or embellishment only reveals to us the fervent human desire to be assured of life everlasting.

The defeat of death as a one-time magical occurrence, however, is not yet sufficient. It has to be overcome as a force in the universe through the power of renewal and re-enactment. The marvel has to relate directly to the holy man himself in such a way as to reveal the power of pure holiness. We return to the text of 2 Kings 2:1-12:

Before Eliyahu is taken from Elisha in a final parting, he asks him what he can do for him. Elisha requests a double portion of his [Eliyahu's] spirit. Eliyahu declares (2 Kings 2:10) that if Elisha is deemed worthy to witness his departure from the temporal world, his wish would be granted. Elisha *does* witness Eliyahu's departure in a *S'arah,* a whirlwind (2 Kings 2:11); Eliyahu simply disappears. As Josephus relates the story, Eliyahu disappeared so that nobody knew that he died (*Antiquities*, Book IX, 2:2).* Elisha's departure is somewhat different. He dies and get a magnificent funeral and Josephus describes him as a doer of marvellous works "such as were gloriously preserved in memory by the Hebrews." (*Antiquities*, Book IX, 8:6).

That both Eliyahu and Elisha were archetypal holy men is clear from the way Josephus presents their departure from the temporal world as the model for sacred thaumaturges. Even in his sepulchre, Elisha has divine power; his very bones revive a dead man who has been placed in his grave - so declares the text of 2 Kings, 13:20. Josephus preserves the story in much the same form. The message is clear: the power of holiness, expressed in speech *and* in touch, is greater than that of death.

It is apparent that such marvels relating to Eliyahu and Elisha were recorded in the folk-memory through ceremonial re-telling down through the centuries. The claim of gospel writers of the Second Century C.E., of a bodily ascent to heaven by a Jesus in a cloud of glory, after his death, represents thematic expansion of earlier material. Moreover, Chapter 2 of *Acts of the Apostles* offers an extended variation on divine power after death: disciples testify to a re-appearance by a Jesus on Pentecost, fifty days after his reported demise.

It was pointed out earlier that the text, in which life events of the holy men, Eliyahu and Elisha, are recorded, is not very good historical writing. A tale retold within the same generation (875-850 BCE) results in some mixups in detail, including strange switches and transfers. For example, in 1 Kings 19:15, the anointing of Hazael as King of Aram and of Elisha as prophet, is entrusted to Eliyahu. Yet, in 2 Kings 8:13, we see that it is *Elisha* who reveals to Hazael, his vision of Hazael's ascendancy to the throne of Syria. Is this a case of multiple authorship resulting in error of fact? Centuries later, this

---

*The work, *The Antiquities of the Jews*, by Flavius Josephus, was first published in 93 C.E.

very characteristic of switch and transfer is revealed in gospel writings, with all their deficiencies and inadequacies as historiography.

Summary

From this brief survey of variety *within* folklore in the Bible, can some major ideas be extracted? Foremost, perhaps, to even begin to decode the language of the times prior to the Common Era, requires the arresting of a natural tendency to anachronism and retrojection. To transpose and retroject our daily outlook to another era will effectively inhibit comprehension of the thought of another age. It would be something like using an unrecognized currency for purposes of goods exchange. Even within our own "currency" of language exchange, difficulty is encountered when we begin to press for greater exactitude. For instance, we believe that we understand the word "society" as when we comment: "society programs us." We are not quite sure what the collective abstraction "society" refers to, and we might be hard-pressed to analyze it, but we tell ourselves that we understand what it means.

Now, if we do this with one of our everyday terms, what is it we do with a vocabulary and idiom that is totally strange to our ears: "Blood is the seat of life, it cries for vengeance"; "gates of Sheol or city of death"; "Absalom stole the heart of the people?" Usually, we simply ignore such an idiom as a foreign and incomprehensible tongue. Or, we make believe we understand through literal translation and retrojection. We do something similar when we "throw back" or project the image of a large urban center (Birmingham, Akron, Pittsburg) upon encountering the term "city."

To began to comprehend the thought patterns of another culture separated from us by centuries requires exertion. More precisely, it involves the shedding of our own "conceptual spectacles" and donning the lenses of comprehension that another people wore in their attempts to extract meaning from their lives. This would permit examination - rather than summary rejection - of thought-constructs like, "justice requires retribution in kind, for order and stability in the universe." The lens of comprehension would extend to an acceptance of forms of expression as the style of an age, i.e., marvels are a way of expressing wonderment and awe.

This can easily be said, but it is extremely difficult to bring about unaided. We begin to understand the difficulty when visiting another land, ostensibly separated from us only in space, not in time. Our conceptions of such basic commonplaces as city, town, village, take on a different hue and coloration when confronted with a marked geographical contrast. Contrasts in time, over millenia, are doubly marked, so our conceptions of what are considered commonplaces, require very careful formulation.

As may be grasped from this brief overview, the "world"-outlook in which the Bible itself was situated, was one where all of nature embodied good and evil forces, where magic was itself a "natural" force, where myth and marvel were the topics of daily conversation, where one might receive the essence of another through physical contact, or the use of the same clothing, or even by bearing the same name, or that essence can be destroyed by name alteration!

[It may be noted that even in an "advanced" civilization, changes in the *spelling* of a name are believed to be changes in substance: Shirley to Shyrlie or Chyrlee.] How is one to confront such strangeness of expression? One might just as well ask how we confront the mispronunciation of "our" words by a foreigner? Usually through laughter. The price of entry to a different world of consciousness requires the avoidance of literalistic translation or, indeed, any attempt at translation. Instead, would-be comprehension calls for the acknowledgment that a standard of judgment can be altogether different from our own. With greater humility and tolerance, the understanding of our own attempts to extract meaning from our lives will be enhanced and sharpened.

2. Biblical Tradition and the Discovery of Sexual Knowledge

The presentation consists of two asymmetrical parts: the first is a review of anthropological material regarding the origins of sexual knowledge. The second, much shorter, deals with a succinct biblical announcement.

Introduction

There are some things that we think have always been part of human knowledge: the use of fire and the knowledge of how new life is generated. It is difficult for us to imagine a time in human history when human beings were unaware of these simple "facts of life." Ignorance so profound, seems unbelievable. Was there a time when these facts were not known? Are we able to form an image of such a time? What kind of humans were they who did not know such basic facts of life? Imagine, as well, how the respective discoveries of technology on the one hand – represented by fire – and the link between physical union of the sexes, to the procreation of offspring, on the other, came to be.

Most of us have heard how the Titan, Prometheus, brought fire from Heaven to Earth as a gift to Mankind, for which act he was punished by being bound to a rock for eternity. (Less familiar is Genesis 4:22 which indicates that Tubal-Kayin is probably the founder of the smith guild in the working of brass and iron.) The details of the story of the origins of technology concern us less than the attempted explanation of a transition from helplessness – in the face of overpowering natural forces – to the beginnings of mastery over nature, whose end is not yet.

Consider now, the transition from total obliviousness of the connection between physical union of the sexes and generation, the connection between instinctive gratification of a transient passion with its subsequent result. How and when did that come about? It came about – as does most human knowledge – gradually, and with much misinformation and fanciful story-telling and errors: the clouding-over of objective fact because of unawareness of human limitation, i.e., the inevitable distortions of the subjective senses.

To what source do we go to find out about earliest human existence? Essentially, there are only two sources: physical remains, which require decoding a story told in rock and stone; and the other source is in ethnology, folk-lore and myth – the story told *by* a story, *within* a story – the expression of collective memory. (Ancient myth tried to explain important aspects of existence by involving human beings with divine beings; it simply took-for-granted a vital connection between the two. That is hard for us to fathom today.)

Sir James Frazer, among others, collected the lore that peoples all over the world have told in story, ballad, song, and epic. In the absence of the techology of writing, exact repetition and ritualization were cultivated and relied upon to preserve authenticity. Far from being useless, such stories reveal ancient conceptions regarding nature, and conceptions about human origins. What does the story contained in folk-lore tell us of the origins of sexual knowledge (which, in turn sheds light on the origins of the family?) There is heavy reliance on the studies of Edwin Hartland, in the seminal work, *Primitive Paternity,* Vol. 1.[1]

Some Conceptions Concerning How Pregnancy Was Produced in the Animal World

Essentially, human being told themselves stories or made empiricist observations. These are basic human methods. Forces of nature were apparently involved. Vegetation appeared to require only moisture to reproduce itself. Consider the line from Shakespeare in the play *Antony and Cleopatra.* In Act II, Scene VII, Lepidus says: "Your serpent of Egypt is bred now out of your mud by the operation of your sun; so is your crocodile." Rain has been thought to have begotten children as have the sun's rays. Apis, the sacred bull of Memphis, was believed to have been begotten by a blaze of light from the moon. Wind has caused birth, according to human theorizing. Hera, wife of Zeus, conceived Haephaistos by inhaling the wind. In Longfellow's poem *Hiawatha*, the maiden, Winona, received the west wind and bore Hiawatha. On the Isle of Women in the China Sea and on an isle off the coast of Sumatra where no men lived, it was believed that the women were fertilized by the wind (like the legendary Amazons). Conception also occurred by bathing and by swallowing fish or worms, so ran the human record.

In Israel, before the founding of the modern State, the shrines of St.

George enjoyed a reputation among Muslims and Christians alike regarding the effect of hot springs vapours. When barren women came to the springs, when the hot air steamed up, they believed themselves visited and impregnated by the saint. The anthropological evidence indicates that mankind has evolved from a state socially and mentally *more* backward than that of the lowest extant savages, of whom there are fewer and fewer in the world, taking neoliths as the standard for the savage state.

What was the state? The notion or dream of shape-shifting was not an extra-ordinary occurrence but an ordinary incident. Why? Because it was taken-for-granted that magic – one of the "laws" of nature – was a force in the world, with everything dependent upon volition. Mere *expression* of a wish like "get well" or even just formation of it was sufficient to obtain the result – depending, of course, on *mana*. The might of verbal charm or curse was a commonplace of folklore. Even *this* kind of charm could produce pregnancy.

Thus, in the ideational structure of early human culture, with regard to the producing of animal pregnancy, there was no thought of a connection between pregnancy and the physical union of the sexes. Instead, reciprocal influence between events in the heavens and those on earth, served as the connection. The belief in a connection between events in heaven and on earth underlies the persistence and popularity of the lore of astrology. So, reciprocal influences were the foundation of the magical practices that were to result therefrom.

If we needed more evidence of the absence, or even a passing thought, of a connection between pregnancy and physical union, we have only to consider the inexhaustible and world-wide tales of supernatural births.[2]   In Greek mythological explanations, Danae conceived Perseus through a shower of gold (presumbly the sun's rays). Bacchus - son of Jupiter and Proserpine - was destroyed by Titans. His heart was pounded up and given in a drink (by Jove) to Semele, and he was born again of Semele. Pregnancy was often attributed to eating and drinking. In a rather late Farsee tradition (the ninth century C.E.), Zarathustra's mother drank homa-juice and cow's milk infused with God's spirit and glory, and thus conceived him. Even later, Jenghiz Khan's mother was impregnated by a divine glance, while the Aztec god, Quetzalcoatl, resulted from his mother's having swallowed a jade or turquoise, thereby becoming impregnated. Stones came to be believed as a substance that could fructify women; in much later development, stone phalli were actually used in temples. The assortment of references is not intended to amuse but to give an idea of the distribution of the theory of supernatural birth. Awareness of these speculative theories should not make us smug about our own fancifulness. If anything, the human record should instruct us in humility, that we are not as all-knowing as we think we are.

As one traces through the collection of tales and stories concerning reproduction, changes and development may be noted. The story-types begin to reveal a gradual, nascent awareness regarding sexual union. Births occur because of transmigration of forms and reincarnation. For instance, among the aborigines in NW Australia, a tribal belief was held that a previously existing soul was engendered by conveyance into the body of the mother, a result only to be effected through the instrumentality of the medicine-man. Common to the Greeks was the idea of swallowing a portion of the bodily substance of another and thus, becoming the parent of the hero in one of his rebirths.

The Babylonian god, Tammuz (as well as his counterparts Attis in Lydia and Adonis in Syria), was born because a pomegranate was laid in the bosom of his mother, the nymph Nana. Here we see the effect of imitative magic, a potent, self-evident force, in the ideational structure of a stage in human development. A similar example of imitative magic was the practice in medieval Ruthenia of placing unripe hen's eggs within a woman to induce fertility. In India, Buddha, in the form of a white elephant, was said to have entered his mother's womb. The idea of fully-formed offspring or parthenogenesis is found in the Greek story of the goddess Athena's birth. Parthenogenesis became a respected theory and was long held to be possible; even until the 17th century, it was still a matter of controversy. So, too, was the theory of spontaneous generation. No less than Augustine in his *City of God*, offered spontaneous generation of animals on remote islands as explanation of the repopulation of the earth after the Flood of Noah.

Let us summarize up to this point: It took hundreds and thousands of years for the process of sexual generation to be understood. *All* conception seemed marvelous at a certain point in human development, and tales of unusual conception were a further step on the road *away* from incomprehensibility. (This is not as curious as appears at first.) Left entirely to ourselves, i.e., without cultural transmission, it is impossible for us to link cause and effect, especially when – as in the case of reproduction – the effect is so distant from the cause. Immediate results alone strike animals and primitives as connected with their antecedents. We are not shocked at the idea that animals behaving instinctively do not comprehend cause and effect. While it is more difficult to imagine humans as equivalent in mental development to animals, sadly the story of human awareness of cause and effect has indicated a slow and gradual process of development.

Today, the empirical observation that pollen is carried by the wind to fructify flowers is a commonplace. Yet, it is instructive for us to note that natives in Mesopotamia and Egypt - for thousands of years - brushed the pollen of the male palm tree on the ovaries of the female date. Is there a substantive difference between the practices then and now? Empiricistically, the ancients "knew" that the process was necessary – because of a theory of magic – to prevent disease or an evil spirit. Only in this century was there understanding that the process they were assisting in was a sexual one: artificial fertilization. Even in Twentieth Century England, hops growers had to be instructed not to root out male hops plants as useless; they had to be persuaded that wind-borne pollen of the male plant was necessary for full ripening of the female fruit. Even in this sophisticated and advanced century, full understanding is limited by an obliviousness.

Divine Births

The lack of knowledge of biological function can, perhaps, best be evidenced by the involvment of gods in the occurrence of virgin births in all cultures. That *all* births were - at one time - the result of divine visitation, is highly significant for the development of the family structure and for the social organization known as matriarchy. Women were looked at as mysterious creatures who had the secret of life and, because they could bring forth produce from their own bodies, in a later age, they were thought to be effective seed-sowers and planters of the soil. Having the secret of life conferred on them through divine knowledge, women became founders of the earliest forms of social organization.

After awareness of the requirement for physical union of sexes in reproduction came to be disseminated widely, the exact nature of impregnation was constructed out of an amalgam of prior conceptual speculations, ranging from spontaneous generation and including parthenogenesis and impregnation by the spirit of the divine essence. Thus, Church fathers came to insist that a Jesus was born without any physical changes in the body that bore him. In fact, portraits of the Annunciation showed a full-formed babe descending in rays from the outstretched finger of the father or – as in 15th century paintings – Jesus entered the virgin's womb fully formed. It is strikingly consistent that illegitimate children were also viewed as the effect of a purely spiritual connection - but that with demons or incubi, seen only in dreams. For instance, King Arthur's magician, Merlin, was believed to have been spiritually conceived by Satan. There certainly was a difference, however, between commerce with the devil and connection with the divine essence.

Some examples of the connection between a human mother and the divine essence are found in the following: At mid-fourth century C.E., Augustine wrote: "God spoke by the angel and the Virgin was impregnated by the Ear." (Painters represented a hovering dove and ray of light entering Mary's ear - recalling earlier versions of light as the source of transmission of essence.) In the Muslim tradition, the miraculous conception occurred as a result of the angel Gabriel's breathing upon Mary's womb (reminiscent of God breathing into Adam). The statement by Lactantius, who wrote in the period just prior to Nicaea (300-317 C.E., is very revealing. Along with the early Church father, Eusebius, he gives us authoritative information on Church doctrine.

As indicated in his words, Lactantius accepted the early theory of conception by the wind and air, but added his own creative gloss:

*"And so, that Holy Spirit of God coming down from
heaven chose the holy virgin by means of whose
womb He would make his way among us. She,
filled completely with the divine Spirit, conceived
Him, and without any contact with a man her
virginal womb was suddenly fruitful.*

[Lactantius goes on to complain against those
who find this strange.]

*Now if is known to all that certain animals
are wont to conceive by the wind and air
(Cf. Vergil, Georgics 3.2 74) why should
anyone think it strange when we say that
the Virgin was made pregnant by the Spirit of
God to whom whatever He wishes is easy?"[3]*

The Biblical Account of the Genesis of Sexual Knowledge

Now, let us turn to the Biblical account of the primeval state: the
begining of life on earth. What follows is an interpretation of the story of
Adam and Eve as the birth of awareness of how life is generated. It is a
story of a revolution in thought processes, the genesis of what is called
science: the linking of cause and effect.

A prefatory note is necessary: Fundamentalists and radical critics
alike make one common error: reading the Bible as a history book or
interpreting it literalistically. A huge pitfall awaits those who consider
Adam and Eve in the purely historical sense. That they indicate an historical epoch in the development of the consciousness of human beings
seems more likely. However, it seems apparent that the story of Adam
and Eve is *not* biography, but moral teaching through allegory. As was
said earlier regarding Prometheus and Tubal-Kayin, the details are less
important than the explanation of a transition from helplessness, to the
beginnings of the mastery of tool construction and use. So it is with the
story of Adam and Eve, where we view the birth of knowledge of self as
an overcoming of another *kind* of helplessness.

How long did it take for the human animal to discover the connection between physical union of the sexes and procreation of the species? In its wonderfully simple and straightforward way, the biblical narrative begins - not at the obcure paloeolithic past, but at the dawn of consciousness and self-awareness; it begins with a proclamation of the discovery and origin of sexual knowledge which occurs within historical time. Genesis 3:7 has one simple sentence: "And the eyes of them both were opened and they knew they were naked." This is the first indication of human awareness. In Chapter 4:1, it states: "And Adam *knew* Havah (Eve) his wife and she conceived and bore Kayin (Cain)." What did he *know*? The new knowledge, the connection between physical union and the birth of a life. That is what was *new*.

The setting is not prehistory, eons ago, but in an historical epoch, when mankind had evolved to the point of consciousness of self, and to the knowledge of physical reproduction. Sometimes, the usual allegorical interpretations of the story tend to obscure this equally important understanding. For instance, the gist of the story is often given as an explanation of human mortality, i.e., the introduction of death into the world. Some questions may be raised about this interpretation, often referred to as the "Fall of Adam."

Was man indeed immortal before the "fall" and then punished with the loss of immortality? This interpretation seems woven into the main body of the story inasmuch as a Tree of Life and a Tree of Death are mentioned in Genesis 2:9, 16. Did the loss of immortality result from eating of the fruit of the Tree of Death by mistake? (The Tree of Life was not forbidden to the couple, as was the Tree of Knowledge alone.) This story about the origins of death seems to be tendentiously theological. Indeed, an important question turns on the claims of Christianity. After the death sentence is passed on Adam and Havah (Eve), Christian exegesis asserts that death has been conquered by the provision of a *second* Adam to remove the sin of the first Adam. One hardly knows how to respond to this plausible claim, except to question the historicity of both the second Adam *and* the first Adam. If one holds to an historical first Adam, there is no illogic in an historical person who is referred to as a second Adam.

To return to the tale of Eden, the plain, unadorned text seems clear regarding the "new knowledge":

> *"And when the woman saw that the tree*
> *was good for food... and that the tree was*
> *to be desired to make one wise, she took*
> *of the fruit thereof, and did eat; and she*
> *gave also unto her husband with her, and*
> *he did eat. And the eyes of them both*
> *were opened and they knew that they*
> *were naked... And when God called*
> *to the man asking 'where are you?'*
> *he replied: 'I heard your voice... and*
> *I was afraid because I was naked; and I hid myself.*
> *And God said: 'Who told you that you were naked?'"*

(Genesis 3:6,7; 9-11)

The story form makes the tale easy to grasp since it does not involve the process of abstraction. It also exemplifies individualness and not the collectivity called "humanity." That is both its strength and its deficiency. Its strength because, by implication, it conveys the idea of the importance of a *single* human being as distinguished from an amorphous mass collectivity; moral teaching then becomes possible to develop. Its deficiency, because there is the tendency for us to personalize the story, to literalize it, and to reduce it to ordinary and believable historical occurrence, or to trivialize it. (Witness how an "apple" got into the story, a telling illustration of how lore is developed.) In other words, it is viewed as an actual piece of history even while its message becomes beclouded.

Instead, the story of Adam and Eve provides us with an ancient tale, a succinct summary of mankind's awareness of the connection between the union of the sexes and procreation. More powerfully, with one sweep, the statement – that "their eyes were now opened and they knew that they were naked" – explodes all the tales of parthenogenesis and wonderful births circulating as solemn explanatory theory. For that tremendous and momentous advance in human knowledge – marking the end of naive ignorance – humanity stands in eternal debt.

Notes

[1] Edwin S. Hartland, *Primitive Paternity: The Myth of Supernatural Birth in Relation to the History of the Family.* First published London: The Folklore Society, LXV, 1909. Kraus Reprint Ltd. 1967.

[2] Supernatural birth stories "originated in the non-recognition...of the physical relation between father and child." Hartland, p. v.

[3] From Book IV, Chapter 12, "On Virginial Birth," The Divine Institutes. Trans. by Sr. Mary Francis McDonald OP, Washington, DC. The Catholic University of America Press, 1964, p. 269

3. The Story of Cain and Abel: An Amalgam of Two Purposes: An Account of Economic Warfare And an Account of a Bulwark Against Wanton Murder

Genesis, Chapter 4

A free adaptation of Genesis Chapter 4 is presented at the outset so that details, essential to the interpretation, do not get lost or overlooked. A word about translations of names--which distort through orthographic rendering and pronunciation--is necessary. In the following adaptation, names are not translated but are presented, as given in the original Hebrew text, in transliterated form, in order to convey a particular meaning, as in *Kayin* (a smith). Many seem unaware that the term *God* represents a translation of YHWH or YH or that an even more recent translation of the ancient designation, YHWH, is *The Lord*. Even though it is widely employed, it is considered less than satisfactory, hence, the consonantal letters YHWH alone are used here.

Verses 1-2: And the man knew Ḥavah (Eve), his wife, and she conceived and gave birth to Kayin (Cain) and said: 'I have gained a man with the help of YHWH.' She gave birth again, this time to his brother Hevel (Abel). Hevel became a shepherd, while Kayin was a worker of the soil.

Verses 3-5: In the course of time, Kayin brought some of his crops as an offering to YHWH. Hevel also offered some of the first-born of his flock, from the choicest ones. YHWH paid heed to Hevel and his offering, but to Kayin and his offering, He paid no heed. Kayin became much distressed and his face fell.

Verses 6,7: And YHWH said to Kayin, 'why are you distressed, and why is your face fallen? Surely, if you do right, there is uplift. But if you do not do right, sin is the demon crouching at the door. It lusts after you, yet you can be its master.'

Verse 8: And Kayin *said* [something] to his brother Hevel...[sic]. Then, when they were in the field, Kayin set upon his brother Hevel, and killed him.

Verses 9-12: And YHWH asked Kayin, 'Where is your brother, Hevel?' And he said, I do not know. Am I my brother's keeper?' Then He said, 'What have you done? The voice of your brother's blood *cries out* to me from the ground! Now, you are cursed from the soil *by the Earth* that had to *open its mouth* to take your brother's blood from your hand. If you till the soil, it shall no longer yield of its strength to you; you will be *unsettled and restless* on the earth.'

Verses 13,14: And Kayin said to YHWH, 'my sin [punishment] is greater than I can bear. Since you have banished me this day from the soil, and I must avoid your presence and become a restless wanderer on earth, anyone who meets me may kill me.'

Verses 15, 16: Then YHWH said to him: 'Therefore, if anyone kills Kayin, seven-fold vengeance shall be taken on him.' And YHWH *placed a mark* on Kayin so that none who meet him should kill him. And Kayin left the presence of YHWH and dwelt in the land of Nod, to the east of Aden.

Verses 17, 18: Kayin knew his wife and she conceived and bore Ḥanokh. And he then founded a city and named the city after his son Hanokh [Enoch]. To Ḥanokh was born Irad, and Irad had a son Meḥuyael, and Meḥiyael had a son Metushael, and Metushael begot Lamekh.

Verses 19-22: And Lemekh wedded two women. The first one's name was Adah and the other one's name was Tzillah. Adah gave birth to Yaval, who was the ancestor of all those who live in tents and who breed herds. The name of his brother was Yuval; he was the ancestor of all who play the lyre and the pipe. As for Tzillah, she bore Tubal-Kayin, who *forged all implements of copper and iron.* And the sister of Tubal-Kayin was Naamah.

Verses 23, 24: And Lemekh said to his wives: 'Adah and Tzillah, hear my voice, wives of Lemekh, and give ear to my speech. I have killed a man for wounding me and a lad for bruising me. [According to tradition, these were Kayin and Tubal-Kayin.] If Kayin is avenged seven times, then for Lemekh it shall be seventy-seven times.'

Introduction

In this presentation of an account of a bulwark against wanton murder, and an account of economic warfare, an interpretation of the Cain and Abel story is offered that relies heavily on sources external to the Bible. Biblical narrative is regarded as moral teaching, presented in the form of singular personalities; it is *not* an historical or collective account that focuses on events and their causes, nor on chronological sequence. Yet, some will persist in asking logical-historical questions of the following type: "Of whom was Cain afraid, when he says 'every man will kill me,' if Cain and Abel were the first people on the earth?" This kind of understanding is the result of not moving beyond the confines of a Sunday School education with a skewed perspective. Even the great folk-lorist, Sir James G. Frazer with his massive contribution to knowledge, made this kind of basic error:

"...God affixed the mark to Cain in order to save him from assailants, apparently forgetting that there was nobody to assail him, since the earth was as yet inhabited only by the murderer himself and his parents. Hence by assuming that the foe of whom the first murderer went in fear was a ghost instead of a living man, we avoid the irreverance of imparting to the deity a grave lapse of memory little in keeping with divine omniscience."[1]

This stretches literalistic interpretation to the breaking point! It is a prime example of transplantation and free intermixture of modes of thought: from the moral to the historical setting. The moral story is expressed in singular lives. The historical deals with a collectivity of persons, movements, and events. Frazer has here committed a common, but grievous error of confuting the two. The remainder of this essay is an argument against just such a reading of a biblical story: moral teaching is *not* to be translated into history! Caution is, therefore, raised against literalistic interpretation of a moral tale, expressed in the singular. For, it is vain to hope that one can freely transplant *modes* of interpretation (i.e., murder is wrong) hoping that a precise historical accounting will be the result of such an operation. As was indicated, in the presentation here, there is reliance on material culled from a variety of sources of folklore, to reconstruct the design and significance of an ancient tale.

Ancient Beliefs About Blood

Blood was seen as both life itself *and* as pollutant. In the book of Deuteronomy 12:23, we find the expression, *"HaDam hu hanefesh,"* "Blood is the Life." But the term *nefesh*, translated as life, is also one of the terms later employed for the concept of "soul." Indeed, in the *Iliad* of Homer, there is an alternation between blood and soul.

That is to say, blood is the same as spirit or ghost, and the blood of a victim of murder endangers the murderer by calling for vengeance. In verse 10 of the biblical story, Hevel's blood cries out for vengeance. Blood cries, translates to "the spirit cries." Thus, many centuries later in time, God is called upon to hearken to the blood that cries to him (2 Maccabees 8:3).

Yet, blood is also a contaminant or pollutant. In Number 35:31 we read: "You shall take no ransom for the life of a murderer that is guilty of death..." In Verse 33, it goes on to say: "You shall not pollute the land wherein you dwell; for blood pollutes the land, and no expiation can be made for the land, for the blood that is shed therein, but by the blood of him that shed it."

How is it that blood is both life *and* pollutant? Recall that folklore is a multi-layered accumulation, like language, involving different ways of expressing an idea. To ask "which way is the right one?" involves us in a tangle of our own creation.

As long as blood lay exposed to the air, then, it continued to call for vengeance. Such a statement appears in the book of Job 16:18:

> *"O earth cover not my blood and let my cry have*
> *no resting place."*

Yehezkel exclaims in Ezekiel 24:6-8:

> *"Woe to the bloody city.. for her blood is in the*
> *midst of her; she set it upon the bare rock; she*
> *poured it not on the ground to cover it with dust, that*
> *it might cause fury to come up to take vengeance..."*

The blood calling for vengeance is most graphically depicted in the legend surrounding the murder of the (non-literary) prophet, Zechariah, at the time of the siege of Jerusalem by the Babylonians in the sixth century BCE. Zechariah had been killed in an earlier century, (2 Chronicles 24:20-22) and as the legend has it, his blood boils on the Temple floor and refuses to be stanched. Nebuzaradan, the conquering general of Jerusalem, slays hundreds of youths, in order to quiet the blood of the prophet. It ceases its seething only after he speaks to it: "Zechariah, Zechariah, do you desire the destruction of the whole people?"

This same theme is expressed by Aeskylos in the Oresteia, where the blood of the murdered king, Agamemnon, cannot be wiped out. Similarly, one may recall Lady Macbeth who – after murdering King Duncan – constantly rubs her hands as she exclaims: "Out damned spot! Yet, who would have thought the old man to have had so much blood in him. Here is the smell of blood still: all the perfumes of Arabia will not sweeten this little hand."

Many tribes tried to avoid the spilling of blood directly on the ground; the attempt was to catch it in vessels on altars, ostensibly because expiation was required if spilled on the ground. The question is why? There are some related questions as well: Why was stoning the preferred means of capital punishment? Or, as in the manner of execution of royalty by the Mongols, why was smothering in a blanket employed? The answer lies in the world-outlook of the particular period and the stage of development attained. The Earth was a powerful Divinity that could be defiled by the spilling of blood upon it. Thus viewed, everything begins to fall into place. Now, what was the punishment for such pollution of a deity [the Earth]?

The Punishment

Blood spilled on the ground renders the soil barren; seed will not germinate nor bear fruit. In 2 Samuel 1:21, David utters a curse on Mount Gilboa, where Shaul and Yonathan (Saul and Jonathan) were slain: neither rain nor dew is to fall on the mount, nor is it to yield any produce. Indeed, one can still see its bleakness and barrenness today, on the outskirts of Beit Sh'an. In Sophokles's play, *Oedipus* says that all of Thebes suffers infertility, as a result of his having slain his father, Laius, albeit accidentally. Blight or sterility is the penalty for bloodshed, with the same idea being found in Aeskylos, in the

Eumenides. What is common in each of these illustrations is a world-outlook that employs *fright* as a deterrant to the shedding of blood. Thus, in Genesis 4:11-12, we read the curse on Kayin:"Now you are cursed from the soil by the Earth that opened her mouth to receive your brother's blood... you will be unsettled and restless on the earth."

It may be noted that *God* has not cursed Kayin; the Earth has done so, and will refuse to yield him his produce. Personifications express the point directly and fearsomely: The deity, Earth, opens her mouth to receive the blood that was shed (Gen. 4:11). Moreover, from the ground, the blood "cries out," meaning that there are vengeful ghosts. (The same idea is expressed in Aeskylos's *Agamemnon*.) Since a murderer poisons the *source* of life (i.e., the Earth) and jeopardizes the food supply of an entire community, he is infected, and has to be quarantined or excluded, as his very touch may cause blight.

Thus, the penalty of restlessness (Gen. 4:12) makes sense. (Nod means unsettled or wandering.) There were perils in travelling on unguarded and unprotected roadways as one reads in Judges 5: "caravans ceased and wayfarers went by devious routes." No doubt, this is probably what Kayin was referring to when he said: "Anyone who meets me may kill me" (Gen. 4:14). (Kayin was presumed to have been killed by his great, great, great grandson, Lemekh, who was blind (Gen.4:24).

In the stories of Orestes and Oedipus, a slayer of a kinsman must suffer banishment under Greek law. In Plato's *The Laws* (886 C-D), if a murderer was on the sea, and was cast away on the land where his crime had been committed, he could stay – only so long until another ship came to carry him away. However, there was a proviso; he had to keep his feet in sea-water in order to dilute the poison that he would otherwise instill into the earth. If there was to be retrial of his case, it would have to be held aboard a ship in the harbor. One may note the lengths to which a society would go to avoid contaminating the Earth!

From the foregoing, it is clear that the ancient bulwark against wanton murder was rooted in myth and magic. But why? The science of the day had to be expressed in the language of the times, i.e., transformed to a literary level. Moreover, it had to engage the current theory of the way the universe worked, namely, through the magical transference of qualities. The then current theory or explanation of the universe involved the literary device of myth: the *Earth* was a divinity. Personifications or anthropomorphizations are, then, easily understood: the Earth "opens her mouth," there are vengeful ghosts or spirits in "crying" blood, the land can become polluted.

Thus, in the absence of a developed habit of reason, we can see that fright may have been needed as a barrier against the easy taking of human life. In our complacent sense of superiority (engendered by the magic in the phrase "twentieth century"), we may regard this constructed prop of revulsion against wanton murder as pure superstition; instead, we might view it as a particular stage of slow and laborious development of our forebears, a process of development in which we, ourselves, are very much involved.

Significance of the Mark of Kayin (Genesis 4:15-16)

The analysis of the *mark* placed on the forehead of Kayin serves as the bridge connecting the two parts of this essay. Generally, the phrase "mark of Kayin" (Cain) conveys, at least, a sense of foreboding, the popular interpretation of this mark on the forehead being that it represents a badge of shame. In medieval Christendom, the Jewish badge on clothing was considered as just such a mark inasmuch as Jews, collectively, were murderers. One may note that branding used to be common for offenders and slaves, and in 17th Century America, blasphemers were branded with a "B"; one may also recall Hawthorne's famous "Scarlet Letter" (A) sewn onto a costume. In 1822 in England, Parliament formally abolished the custom of branding an "F" on a felon's cheek. In ancient Babylonia, the expression "to clean the brow" [of a mark] meant to "emancipate." It seems evident, then, that there would be a tendency to react to the phrase "mark of Kayin" in a negative way.

Yet, the Bible story appears to suggest that the mark was a sign of protection! For instance in Ezekiel 9:4, one reads: "Set a mark on the foreheads [of the faithful.] Come not near any man upon whom is the mark." This may indicate something else entirely. Devotees of a god often bore distinctive marks such as circumcision or an in-sealing in the flesh. For instance, in ancient Egypt, sacral tatooing was practiced as was the ritual shaving of the head and, of course, Christians perform the ritual of baptism, as a means of devoting the individual to the Divine. But, other hypotheses are offered as well.

Sir James Frazer suggested that the blood (i.e., ghost) of a murdered man haunts the perpetrator of the murder and demands vengeance. Hence, "The mark of Cain may originally have represented a mode of disguising a homicide or rendering him so repulsive or formidable in appearance that his victim's angry ghost would either not know him or at least give him a wide berth."[2] This idea of haunting the perpetrator of murder represents a composite substratum of belief. Even public executioners had to take precautions against the ghosts of the executed (i.e., against "blood for blood") by incisions on the executioner's body. Similarly, Indian tribal warriors, who had just tortured a man to death, also marked their bodies, and set up a din and loud racket in the camp to scare the ghost away.

The belief in a ghost seemed fairly widespread. In Plato (*The Laws*) , a homicide had to leave his country for a year, until the wrath of the ghost died down, and purificatory ceremonies were performed. The banishment was necessary because the ghost would be enraged at the sight of the homicide walking about freely. Similarly, the Omaha Indians prescribed a stringent ritual for a murderer who was spared by the victim's kinsmen. He was banished from the interior of the camp, could not eat warm food, nor raise his voice, nor look around. By contrast, some tribes had the practice of marking a murderer, in order to represent a pecuniary payment (rather than a bloody one), for the deed committed; this meant that the ghost could have no further claim!

There is a common element in all of these illustrations: *dread*. It is Frazer's major contention that "the seclusion of [manslayers] from society is dictated by no moral aversion to their crime; it springs from ... dread of the ghost by which the homicide is supposed to be pursued and haunted."[3]

It will be recalled that in the Biblical story, while it is the blood of the victim which endangers the murderer by calling out for vengence, the term "blood" alternates in meaning with spirit or ghost, or with: "The blood is the life," as in Deuteronomy 12:23.

So far, we have spoken of "the mark" as an indicator of shame or protection, the former being a corruption, while the latter [protection] was more likely. In point of nomenclature, *kayin* in Hebrew and Arabic is equivalent to *smith*. (In 1 Samuel 13:19, a *smith* is labelled a *ḥarash* which means *crafter*.)

The smith - who worked with metals and forge - was believed to be under God's protection, and had semi-sacred status. (That status was enjoyed by the Titan, Prometheus, who brought down fire from heaven to earth.) Injury to a smith was to be requited seven-fold as in the Song of Lemekh (Genesis 4:24).

Was "the mark," then, a guild-sign of metal workers, signifying sacrosanct status? It is most tempting to think so! Genesis 4:22 may be recalled here: Kayin's great, great, great, grandson (Tubal-kayin) forged all implements of copper and iron; he was the ancestor of all metal-workers. It may be pointed out that, in the 1890's, Sudanese nomadic smiths wore a cross-shaped mark on the brow. Evidently, what appeared to be an ancient penalty (i.e. wandering) was, in fact, a guild-characteristic of the itinerant craft of smithing. The guild was composed of "*Kenim*" or Tinkers, who moved from village to village servicing the hardware needs of the residents by metal-working. Thus, we come now to an early account of economic warfare, expressed in the literary style of the story of Cain and Abel.

The Smith Versus the Herder

In the usual interpretation of the biblical story, the moral teaching about murder is of prime importance; the murderer is a farmer and the victim a keeper of sheep. Later visions preserve the idyllic nature of pastoral life, with the image of the shepherd being the ideal: Abel, Jacob, Moses, David, Amos are all shepherd-types. Even God is portrayed as the perfect shepherd; one need only recall the opening lines of Psalm 23; that recollection is ample evidence of the popularity of the calling. In point of nomenclature, the Hebrew name, *Hevel,* refers to a herder. (In Arabic, the name appears as *Ibl* and in Syriac, *Habla*, herder or swineherd. The name, *kayin*, and the plural, *Kenim*, referred to smiths.)

We meet the Kenim or Kenites (not to be confused with Kenaanites) in Numbers 10:29 where they are associated with the Midianites. In Numbers 24:21, they are found with the Amalekites – a clear indication of the itinerant nature of their work: forging metal tools and weapons. In Judges 1:16, we learn that the father-in-law of Moses (Yithro) belonged to the Kenites who were attached - perhaps in an economic way – to the Midianites. In 1 Samuel 15:6, King Shaul (Saul) is on a military expedition against the Amalekites, and he sends word to the Kenites to depart from the Amalekite camp, lest they too be smitten in battle. From these internal references, it is clear who the Kenites were, and what the nature of their occupational activity was: itinerant smiths. The question is: what do these descendants of Kayin reveal to us about the nature of the ancient struggle between Kayin and Hevel?

In the second millenium BCE, there are tales of rivalry between shepherd and farmer, in Sumerian national epics.[4] For example, in the altercation between the cattle herder, *Enten*, and his brother, *Enmesh* who is a crop grower, each one recites his merits and accomplishments to the god *Enlil*. He chooses Enten, the herder, as steward of the Divine Estate. (Compare with Genesis 4:3-5.) Another Sumerian tale treats of a quarrel between the god of cattle and the god of grain, with each extolling his achievements and belittling the other. (Indeed, crop growers have different needs than cattle raisers. Even among animal breeders, quarrels over pasturage will arise, since cattle-ranchers have different requirements for their animals than sheep-herders do. Such quarrels were a familiar story throughout history.) In all these illustrations, the common element is the rivalry and quarrel. Now, in literature and drama, there is a genre known as the debate. The rivals can be the sea and the land, spring and summer (as in Shakespeare's *Love's Labour Lost*), the pomegranate and the apple (as in Aesop), or members of rival trades or economic modes of existence. As found in Genesis 4:8, the debate is a silent one exept for one curious reference: "And Kayin *said* to his brother Hevel..."

The ellipsis is in the original, with a strange break-off in the sentence. In the very next verse, Kayin kills Hevel. What was said between the two? Did Hevel extol his achievements while belittling Kayin's? We can only surmise, but we do know that Kayin's anger was aroused. What is strange in the whole story is that Kayin is represented as a farmer, even though his name means "smith." This may be a result of dim reflections, and the blending of tales and traditions from a polymorphic texture. As Karl Jaspers has said: "We can ask primal questions but we can never stand near the beginning." A reconstruction is offered, not of the singular personalities of the two principals, but of the implications in terms of collective groups.

The Story of Economic Warfare
Between an Old Order and A New Order

The old order is the pastoral life. What is important to it are water, pasture, freedom of access to the land. Its tools are natural products such as sticks, stones, rope woven from animal material. Pastoral life marks out a territory for itself and follows a seasonal route of movement, much like the migrant agricultural workers who follow the growing season. At the end of what is called the Stone Age, during a period of transition, there is the beginning of the use of metals among humans (Genesis 4:22 on Tubal-Kayin), and these new substances are somewhat awesome and over-powering. New occupations appear: mining and metallurgy, as some people begin working with the new substances. They discover that they can make useful products which can be bartered for animals skins and other necessities. These miners and metal-workers are called *Kenim* or Smiths.

Now, the *Kenim* or miners are wanderers by necessity, i.e., searchers for metal, rootless strangers with an air of mystery about them, which renders them untouchable or unapproachable. Sometimes, they are marked with a special sign, indicating membership in a guild; today, we might use badges and uniforms to show distinctiveness. The smith or *kayin*, is an alien, an itinerant tinker, who has a strange technique of smelting and blending metals, superior to weaving strands of rope fibre or wool together. Even the gods and demons cannot resist the tools and weapons forged by the smith. (Recall that the god Haephaistos or Vulcan was a metal-worker.) The smith is generally (and perhaps, necessarily) homeless, and he wanders from village to village, feared and respected. Some illustrations are offered describing the nature of smithcraft:

In Arabia, smiths were wandering types; many were Jewish as, for example, the powerful Qayyinuqa tribe in the vicinity of Yathrib (today known as Medina). In the seventh century, Muhammed warred against this power-ful tribe of Jewish smiths and decimated their ranks. (One may see the name *kayyin* in the designation Qayyinuqa.) Across the Red Sea, in Abyssinia, smithcraft was characteristic of the group called Falashas, a segregated caste considered outsiders, as the term *Falasha* specifies. Similarly, in Central Africa, among the Masai tribe, smiths were relegated to a caste of foreigners, the term *al kononi*, for smith, being considered a dirty word; encounter with the caste brought disaster. In Somaliland, on the coast of the Red Sea, smiths also functioned as magicians and in Africa, in general, the smith came to be regarded as a combination magical worker and shaman. This ambivalent status of the smith – now as an object of respect, now of disdain – is best illustrated by the Siberian Buriat tribe: a benevolent smith is called a *white* smith while a malevolent smith is called a *black*-smith. Indeed, as the Roman poet Ovid asserted, iron and metal came to be viewed as a shield against demons. Thus, iron horse-shoes over a dwelling brought protection; even today, horse-shoes are regarded as symbols of good luck.

In summary, the economic clash between an older and newer way of earning a living results in bloodshed. The use of iron can kill! Fears of bad magic are aroused that farming will not produce crops because of blood pollution. We can see in the traditional story, labelled Cain and Abel, a blending of tales and traditions, a composite substratum or a multi-layered accumulation. In the biblical tale, the smith appears as a farmer in opposition to the sheep herder. Antipathy between crop-grower, cattle-raiser, and herder has its counter-part in all cultures, as does the antagonism between differing modes of living: country-boy and city-slicker, the rural-urban mutual suspicion, the farmer versus the banker, the technologist versus the humanist.

Conclusion

Moral teaching, that is moral demonstration, is best represented in the individual - rather than the collective - life and, therefore, is presented in the singular instance, not the plural, in the language of the Bible. In transposing the particular teaching into an historical understanding, we are lead into grievous error, for this mode of the singular is not actually suited to historical generalization, which draws on collective life, dealing with causes and effects of events, that are social – not individual – in character. Thus, serious error occurs when one simply transplants the identical *mode of thought* and conceptualization – suitable for moral comprehension – onto historical interpretation or the converse. A way of understanding the biblical story of Cain and Abel in historical perspective is to view it as an amalgam of an account of economic warfare and displacement, as well as an account of a bulwark against wanton murder. What *has* happened is always capable of being understood in a different way. As the story is interpreted anew, it becomes new.

Notes

[1] Sir James G. Frazer, "The Mark of Cain," Chapter III, in *Folklore in the Old Testament*. New York: Tudor Publishing Company, 1923, p.45.

[2] Ibid., p.44.

[3] Ibid., p.40.

[4] James B. Pritchard, *The Ancient Near East, An Anthology of Text and Pictures*. Princeton University Press, 1969, pp. 28ff.

4. Biblical Heirs:
Primogeniture or Ultimogeniture?
Leadership Inheritance
in Ancient Israel

Inheritance: The Cause of Classic Struggles

The issue of inheritance and the passing on the mantle of leadership from one generation to the next, accounts for several classic biblical struggles. Some episodes appear as strange when viewed against the time-honored pre-supposition of primogeniture, the right of the first-born to leadership. One encounters the preference of a father and mother for one son rather than another, as was the case with Avraham and Sarah choosing Yitzhak as heir rather than the eldest son, Yishmael (Genesis 21:10-13).[1] Another instance of parental preference was Israel's choice of Yoseph (Joseph), (at the time, the youngest of all his sons) for special consideration (Genesis 37:3-4). Yet Deuteronomy 21: 15-17 clearly states that if there are two wives, the husband is duty-bound to acknowledge the seniority of the actual first-born, regardless of his affections:

> *"If a man has two wives, one loved and other unloved,*
> *and both the loved and the unloved have borne him sons,*
> *but the first-born is the son of the unloved one. When*
> *he wills his property to his sons, he may not treat as first-born*
> *the son of the loved one in disregard of the son of the*
> *unloved one who is older. Instead, he must accept the*
> *first-born, the son of the unloved one, and allot to him a*
> *double portion of all he possesses; since he is the first fruit*
> *of his vigor, the birthright is his due."*

The question which is the concern of this essay is: was this duty honored in the dawn of Hebrew history? It is suggested that the first-born according to nature was not always the first-born in the sight of God.

Several episodes bear on the question raised. One concerns the birth of twins – Peretz and Zerah to Yehudah (Judah) – wherein there was doubt as to which one was born first (Genesis 38:27-30). Still another had to do with the cupidity and cunning of the younger son, in which a birthright actually gets sold for a bowl of soup (Genesis 25:29-34). One also reads of a switching of hands over heads at a final blessing, the right hand resting on the head of the junior son and the left hand on the senior. When their father, Yoseph (Joseph) tries to move his father Israel's hands, in order to have the right hand resting on the first born son's head (Manasseh), Israel resists, claiming that his action is predictive of greater glory for the younger son, Ephrayim (Genesis 48:13-21). Perhaps the most complete tale and the one most well-examined, is that of the Heel-Catcher, Yaacov (Jacob), so named, because at birth, he was clutching at the heel of his twin brother, Esau (Genesis 25:26). He later undergoes a name change to Israel.

The Heel-Catcher, Yaacov (Jacob), is portrayed as grasping, crafty, and clever in outwitting his brother Esau and – by the strategy and design of his mother – receives his father's blessing of leadership inheritance (Genesis 27:1-46) Yaacov comes before his near-blind father dressed in an animal skin so that – to the touch – he would feel hairy – like his brother. His father, thus being deceived into believing it is his eldest son, imparts the blessing of the first-born to him. Now, if one were to view this episode as reflective of a more ancient custom of inheritance – that of ultimogeniture or junior-right – it would then appear that the younger son, Yaacov, was entitled to receive his due: the blessing of leadership inheritance. It is the contention here that ultimogeniture or junior right preceded primogeniture (the leadership right of the first-born) in Israelite folklore, and that several narratives in the Bible reveal the collision between the two forms of leadership inheritance. First, however, what is the evidence for the claim that ultimogeniture or junior right was the prevailing custom of leadership and inheritance? There are several strands of evidence appearing as unrelated, that may, however, be connected.

Junior Right the Older Tradition of Leadership

The classic struggle for dominance between Jacob and Esau commences while the twins are still in the womb of their mother, Rivkah (Rebekah) (Genesis 25:22-26). A later Midrashic commentary relates that, while still in his mother's womb, Yaacov yielded his position as the "elder brother" in order to save his mother's life. This gloss, would, of course, reflect the dominance of the institution of primogeniture. The question, nonetheless, remains: why does Yaacov appear as the younger of the twins? for, as Genesis 25:23 declares, in response to Rebekah's entreaty: "Two nations are in thy womb ... and the elder shall serve the younger." Given such a declaration, it suggests the dominance of the custom of junior right, not senior right!

The story of Yaacov's grandchildren, Peretz and Zerah (Sons of Judah), is remarkably similar to that of Yaacov and Esav (Jacob and Esau). In this tale one twin, Peretz, clearly is the first-born, but he is *made to appear* as the junior who somehow – in the words of the attendant midwife – has to "clear a path for himself" and and is given the name *Peretz*, which records that very fact.[2] Again, an urgent question demands response: why does Peretz *appear* to be the younger when he is, in biological fact, the older of the twins? It is significant that Peretz is the ancestor of King David (Ruth 4:18 and 1 Chronicles 2:3-15) and this datum offers the hint of a clue. The chronological leap forward suggests an answer.

In 1 Samuel 16:1, 6ff, the seer Shemuel (Samuel) is instructed to anoint a new king to replace Saul.[3] He appears before Yishai (Jesse) of Beit Leḥem, the father of seven sons, and when he views the eldest son, Eliav, he is convinced that this is the one chosen to wear the crown. Yet, the account relates that Shemuel rejects six of Yishai's sons in turn, and asks for number seven, the youngest, who was not even on the scene (1 Samuel 16:10-13). When the youngest, David, is brought before Shemuel, he is anointed by the seer to be the next king of Israel. That David, the youngest son, was elevated to the throne, probably affected the old tribal tale regarding his ancestor, Peretz, who was presented as a junior, born *first*! This contradiction reflects the struggle between two principles of inheritance as well as two principles of social organization. If the institution of ultimogeniture or junior right was the older tradition, it was *this* legitimacy that was required to justify David's own selection as king.

Even in the selection of David's predecessor as the first ruler (1Samuel 9:17-21), Shaul (Saul) is presented as a representative of the *youngest* tribe, Binyamin[4] (Benjamin) or Ben-yami*m*, the son of old age, the title marking Benjamin as lawful heir. Indeed, the claim of the tribe of Ben-yamim to leadership gets revealed in the struggle between the House of Saul (Benjamin) and the House of David (Yehudah/Judah) (2 Samuel 3:1)[5] (See also Judges 20, 21 regarding the claim of Benjamin to inter-tribal leadership.) Then, too, one may note that David's successor is his number seven son, Shelomoh (Solomon), the youngest, not the oldest surviving son, Adoniyahu, who was number four.

Leadership Inheritance Related to Social Organization

It has been contended that Biblical narratives reflect a struggle between two principles of leadership inheritance, as well as between principles of social organization. What is known about the origins of ultimogeniture? It appears to be related in some way to a matrilineal social structure and has been connected with domestic worship, where the youngest daughter inherits the religious practices in organic association with the homestead. It may also be that the youngest child, by reason of tender age, was less able to fend for itself and required an extra measure of protection. Now, the practice of ultimogeniture was not limited to pastoral social units, typified by the family of Jacob in Ḥarran-Aram, but has been found in migratory agricultural units as well, and even after the unit has settled down more or less permanently. With such permanent settlement, the practice of junior right continued to apply, no matter whether the youngest was a daughter or son, since the youngest was usually the last to leave the homestead and was often the mainstay of aging parents. (See Book of Ruth 4:3-5 for a case of inheritance by a woman.) Most often, it was precisely because the youngest remained latest with the parent, that the youngest became heir to the more or less stable estate. Among some more recent nomadic groups such as Mongols and Turks, there was a permanent heir who was attached to the soil or was a "guardian of the hearth." Similarly, the youngest in the Assam tribes of Burma, was considered the heir and was bound to remain at home to take care of parents.

Now, what is the connection between customs and practices of inheritance, say, ultimogeniture, and the principle of social organization? It has been put forward by several anthropological observers that the matriarchial clan was the dominant form of social organization prior to permanent Israelite settlement in Kenaan, i.e., prior to its adoption of agriculture as an economic base.[6] This is grounded on the theory of close connection between patrilineality and agriculture and land ownership, while the matrilineal social structure was connected with a pastoral (or pre-agricultural) economic base. What should not be overlooked, however, is the *effect* that the *lack* of knowledge and aware-ness of the male role in procreation had, in producing matrilineality and matriarchy in the first place! The revolutionary changeover, as a result of diffusion of knowledge concerning the male contribution to producing offspring, will be considered more fully a little later. For the moment, signs and vestiges of matriarchial social organization are noted.

Survivals of the matriarchial clan structure may be found in linguistic usage: *Umma*, people or nation, is a derivative of the term for mother, *Umm*. *Baten*, commonly taken to mean the belly housing the womb, refers to *clan* and descent through the female line. *Rahim (Rehem)*, the word for womb, expresses kinship. Thus, the key words concerning the idea of kinship, are distinctly those relating to maternity, the uterine bond being the most pronounced and direct.[7]

An historiographic residue of matriarchy may be found in the book of Judges 9:1-6, relating the story of Abimelekh and his plot against his brethren of the House of Gideon, in which 68 sons are murdered. Abimelekh's career was made possible by his mother's kin, i.e., the maternal relationship was the basis of his appeal to them for recognition as king. Other residual pieces of matriarchy may be found in the prerogatives of naming children, exercised by Leah and Rahel (Genesis 29:32-35 and 30:6-8,22).[8] In addition, one notes that in the very marriage arrangements between Yaacov and Lavan's daughters – sometimes referred to as *beena* marriage – it is the clan that claims the children.[9] In Genesis 31:43, Lavan voices the claim of the clan: "The daughters are mine and the children are mine." Even his sister, Rivkah (Rebekah), was under his guardianship. As Genesis 24:53 reveals, Lavan *and* his mother received gifts of precious things to induce them to offer Rebekah in marriage. (It should be noted that the name Lavan is probably an eponym for a social organization, rather than just the name of a single individual unattached to a larger grouping.)

Challenge to the Matriarchial Principle

In the aforementioned illustrations may be seen also the beginnings of a newer type of social organizing principle (patriarchy) parallel to the older matriarchial principle. As Morgan notes in *Ancient Society*: "With property accumulating in masses and assuming permanent forms, with an increased proportion of it held by individual ownership, descent in the female line was certain of overthrow and the substitution of the male line equally assured."[10] The Book of Numbers 27:1-7 then becomes clear: inheritance by women occurs in default of male issue. Where there are no sons, daughters are to inherit an estate.[11] (This also explains Ruth 4:3-5.) Moreover, the preservation of a family inheritance by women is to be maintained as provided for in the legislation of Numbers 36:7-9, i.e., within tribal allottment, rather than to be diffused because of marriage.[12]

It appears that one of the requisite economic conditions for the inheritance principle of ultimogeniture or junior right was a wide territory and sparse population. As these conditions were altered, the custom of junior right came to be disputed. However, even as the custom began to yield, vestiges of the older principle of leadership-inheritance remained concurrent with the newer challenging principle; i.e., the residuum of older matrilineal social units colliding with newer patrilineal ones. Thus, there appeared to be compromises between ultimogeniture and primogeniture, the oldest *and* the youngest receiving double portions of inheritance. For instance, in Deuteronomy 33:17, Yoseph received a two-tribe allottment of land in Kenaan. Was it because of his seniority or his juniority? On the one hand, he was the youngest of Yaacov's ten other sons (his younger brother, Benyamim, being born later, in the land of Kenaan, not in Ḥarran-Aram, where Yaacov had been indentured to his father-in-law). On the other hand, Yoseph was the first-born of his mother, Raḥel who, in turn, was the younger of the two sisters whom Yaacov had married. One cannot be certain whether one principle of inheritance, alone, prevailed. Similarly, in the story of the Stolen Blessing (Genesis 27:1-46), while it is clear that Esau is claiming the inheritance right of a senior, the story itself reveals the collision between two institutional claims. One may also note the prominence of the mother, Rivkah, in the story, a reminder of the older leadership principle and matrilineal social organization.

Another instance of collision between senior and junior right is suggested in the clash between David and his eldest brother. In 1 Samuel 17:28-29, Yishai's oldest son, Eliav, reproaches David for daring to come to the war front to meet the challenge of the Philistine giant Golyat (Goliath).[13] One may interpret this incident as Eliav's brooding over his rejection by the seer, Shemuel, in the light of David's anointment as king (1 Samuel 16:6, 7); even so, this would seem to strengthen the case that junior right had prevailed over senior right!

Basis of the Patriarchial Claim to Sovereignty

There is no mistaking the violent nature of the collision over leadership inheritance in Genesis 35:22. The eldest son of Yaacov, Reuven, takes possession of his father's concubine for which act – according to a later midrashic gloss – the birthright of the senior was withdrawn from him. Be this as it may, one notes the import of taking possession of concubines as part of a larger male awareness. The older social order of matrilineality rested upon the erstwhile (and apparent) "magic" of women in producing young from their bodies. When the male role in sexual reproduction began to be grasped and comprehended, defloration became a means of proving maleness. Indeed, the variety of explanations concerning the origin of the famed *jus primae noctis* (the right of the "first night") rarely mention the sacredness (and perhaps fear) of the act of defloration. Among certain social units, this act was to be performed by a professional – often a priest – since it had certain "holy" connections, i.e., women having the power of creation within their own bodies. With the recognition of creative power within the male, as well as the female, came the rise of patriarchial claims and a contest for control. The taking of a father's concubines, then, was a sign marking the transfer of power and sovereignty, as may be seen in the act of Jacob's son, Reuben, in Genesis 35:22.

Later incidents were even more bold. In 2 Samuel 16:20-22, in the revolt of Prince Avshalom (Absalom) against his father, King David, the Prince takes his father's concubines in a brazen public act! When the revolt is quashed, David stages a counter-demonstration: the concubines are to remain in widowhood, even though their master (David) is alive (2 Samuel 20:3).

In still another illustration of the symbols of sovereignty, 1 Kings 2:17-23 relates an incident regarding the succession to David's throne. Prince Adoniyahu requests of the Queen Mother (Bathsheba), his father's nurse, the Shunamite maiden, Avishag.[14]   This request is viewed by the heir-apparent – Adoniyahu's younger brother, Shelomoh – as a bid for the kingship itself. As Solomon bluntly remonstrates with his mother: "And why do you ask Avishag the Shunamite [the nurse] for Adoniyahu? Ask for him the kingdom also for he is my elder brother..." (1 Kings, 2:17-23). Here, in the reference to "elder brother," one can see the conflict between the institutional claims of ultimogeniture and primogeniture at play.

Summary

What has been contended in this study of leadership-inheritance in ancient Israel is that traces of ultimogeniture or junior right obtain, even after it is formally eclipsed by primogeniture. However, explanations are needed to account for the deviations from primogeniture, the practice as found in the Deuteronomic laws – which came later in point of time than the period of

David and Solomon. The deviations or "violations" are found notably in the stories of Jacob and Esau, Peretz and Zeraḥ, Manasseh and Ephrayim, and in the narratives concerning the kings Saul, David, and Solomon. The biblical interpreters attempted to explain the departures from Deuteronomic legislation through devices such as: peculiarities at birth, viz., the story of Peretz and Zeraḥ, of the preference of the father for a particular son, e.g., Jacob for Joseph, or by the cupidity of the younger son, a Jacob or a Solomon. In the case of David's election to be monarch, there may actually have been a subsequent official scribal rendering of an old tribal narrative to make David's ancestor, Peretz, into the junior twin, in order to fashion a rationale for David's own accession to kingship over his older brothers.

That ultimogeniture was, in fact, the ancient tradition and practice of the early Hebrews goes back in folklore to the earliest beginnings: it is the younger son of the primal couple, Adam and Eve, Hevel (Abel), whose offering is preferred by God to that of his older brother, Kayin (Cain). Indeed, the first-born according to nature is not always the first-born in the sight of God![15] How else explain that the outstanding personalities and leaders in ancient Israel are all juniors? Isaac, Jacob, Ephrayim, Moses, David, Solomon. Given a hoary tradition, there was no need to justify ultimogeniture; that was the way things were! The claimants of junior right were entitled to their inheritance.

Notes

[1] Genesis 21:12: "...whatever Sarah tells you, do as she says, for it is through Yitzhak that offspring shall be continued for you."

[2] Genesis 38:27-30: "When the time came for her [Tamar, mother of Peretz and Zerah] to give birth, there were twins in her womb. While she was in labor, one of them put out his hand, and the midwife tied a crimson thread on it to indicate that 'this one came first.' But, as he drew back his hand, out came his brother; and she declared: "So, you have made a breach for yourself!' And he was named Peretz. Afterwards, his brother followed, on whose hand was the crimson thread; he was named Zerah."

[3] 1 Samuel 16:1: "And YHWH said to Shemuel: 'How long will you mourn for Shaul since I have rejected him as ruling over Israel? Fill your horn with oil and go to Yishai, the Beth Lehemite, for I have provided for a king among his sons."
1 Samuel 16:6-7: "And when they [the sons] came, he (Shemuel) saw Eliav and he said: 'This is surely the anointed one of YHWH.' But YHWH said to Shemuel: 'Don't just look on his appearance or on the height of his stature. I have rejected him. For man looks on outward appearances while God looks within the heart.' "

[4] Genesis 35:18: "But as she [Rahel] was dying, she named him Ben-Oni [son of my sorrow] but his father called him Bin Yamin [son of the right hand.]"

[5] 2 Samuel 3:1: "Now there was long war between the house of Shaul and the house of David; and David grew ever stronger while the house of Shaul became weaker and weaker."

[6] Lewis H. Morgan, "Change of Descent from the Female to the Male Line," Chapter 14 of *Ancient Society*. Cambridge, Mass.: The Belknap Press of Harvard University Press, 1964, pp. 294-303.

[7] See Henry Schaeffer, "Matriarchy," in *The Social Legislation of the Primitive Semites*. New Haven: Yale University Press, 1915, p.4.

[8] See also Judges 13:24 and 1 Samuel 1:20 and 4:21.

[9] See Schaeffer, p.2.

[10] From Morgan, p.294.

[11] Number 27:1-7: "The daughters of Zelophehad, of Manassite family... came forward... and said: 'Our father died in the wilderness... and has left no sons. Let not our

father's name be lost to his clan just because he had no sons. Give us a holding among our father's kin...' And YHWH said to Moshe: 'The plea of Zelophehad's daughters is just; you should give them a hereditary holding among their father's kinsmen; transfer their father's share to them.' "

[12] Numbers 36:7-9: "No inheritance of the Israelites may pass over from one tribe to another, but the Israelites must remain bound each to the ancestral portion of his tribe. Every daughter... who inherits a share must marry someone from a clan of her father's tribe, in order that every Israelite may keep his ancestral share. Thus no inheritance shall pass over from one tribe to another, but the Israelite tribes shall remain bound each to its portion."

[13] 1 Samuel 17:28: "And Eliav his eldest brother heard as he spoke to the men and Eliav was angry at David and said to him: 'Why have you come down here? And on whom have you given the responsibility for those few sheep in the wilderness? I know your presumptuousness...' "

[14] 1 Kings 1:1-4 tells of an interesting experiment in what has come to be known as "osphresiology": the imparting of vigor by physical contact with young persons. (This may be the vestige of an ancient belief in transfer of spirit or energy.) It seems that, in advancing age, David had some blood circulation problems; his body was cold. So, a young maiden from Shunem was brought to him to convey her body heat to him through physical contact. Some refer to this practice as Shunamitism. (It is not an uncommon practice of those who find themselves exposed to harsh weather conditions of the open country, to huddle close to each other for some feeling of warmth.)

[15] See Jeremiah 31:9: "For I am a father to Israel and Ephrayim is my first-born." [Ephrayim was the junior son.]

5. From Pessaḥ to Passover: Passover is Older Than the Exodus

Introduction

The ceremonial practices of a nation frequently help to obscure a historical record, if not to distort it. One of the purposes of "the record" (i.e. record-keepers) is to establish the fact(s): *what* happened? Another is to attempt to pinpoint sequence chronologically: *when* did the facts happen, i.e. in what order? (Without order of precedence, one can only speak mystically, not analytically.) The search for more complex purposes of record-keeping include explanations: On what basis is the record itself to be established, i.e., the validity and reliability of *what* is taken to be evidence. This is no small matter; it actually subsumes all major questions. Other complex questions include: *which* of the facts seem more significant than others or *why* did the facts transpire as they did, to produce the record?

The purpose of ceremonial practice is rather different. In part, it is celebratory or memorializing in the attempt to preserve a tradition. It is also instructional in part: a lesson is implicit – or is made explicit – in the practice. To distinguish between ceremonial practice and historical record is to caution against the exchange of one for the other.

Most commonly, because of an anniversarial observance, the ceremonial practice is interpreted, willy-nilly, as the historical record itself; by virtue of its present-ness, it tends to induce uncritical acceptance and arrests thought and analysis. Then, too, another interchange frequently occurs. Moral teaching is viewed as history (or the record) itself. For instance, in reading of the story of two individuals, one is overpoweringly tempted to think in individual terms, for that is precisely the *mode* of moral thought and instruction! But, it is not the mode of thought in constructing a historical record; that requires the analysis of collective groups and movements. Individualization, from the moral landscape, is unwittingly and, perhaps, unavoidably, transposed to the historical landscape, as when Cain and Abel or Simeon and Levi become merely two individuals and not – as they actually represent – two large collective groups. This kind of unwitting transposition also operates when the date of composition of a biblical book is identified with the events being recorded therein. Simply put, an account and the event it records are not identical occurrences in time. Pessaḥ is a case in point; it preceded the exodus of Hebrews from bondage, as well as the account thereof.

Some curious passages form the background of the analysis "From Pessaḥ to Passover" and are presented here in full:

2 Chronicles 35:17: *"And the children of Yisrael*
that were present kept the pessaḥ at that time [621 BCE]
and the Feast of Matzot seven days, and there was
no Pessaḥ like that kept in Yisrael from the days of
Shemuel the prophet, neither did all the kings of Yisrael
keep such a Pessaḥ as Yehoshiyahu kept... in the
eighteenth year of Yoshiyahu [sic] was this Pessaḥ kept."
[Yehoshiyahu was King of Judah from 638-609 BCE.]

Josephus: *Antiquities of the Jews*, Book III, Chapter 10:5, "Concerning the Festivals." (Original publication date, ca. 93 C.E.)

"In the month of Xanthicus, which is by us called Nissan,
and is the beginning of our year, on the fourteenth day
of the lunar month, when the sun is in Aries... the law
ordained that we should every year slay that sacrifice...
which was called the Pessaḥ and so do we celebrate this
passover in companies, leaving nothing of what we
sacrifice till the day following. The feast of unleavened
bread succeeds that of the passover, and falls on the
fifteenth day of the month and continues seven days..."

Josephus speaks of two distinct holidays: Pessaḥ *and* the feast of unleavened bread as does Chronicles refer to Pessaḥ *and* the Feast of Matzot. The Book of Joshua, which records events of an earlier day, also makes the same distinction (Joshua 5:8, 10):

5:8: *"And it happened that when all the nation*
were circumcised... they remained in their places
in the camp until they were well."
5:10: *"And the children of Yisrael encamped in*
Gilgal, and they kept the pessaḥ on the fourteenth
day of the month at evening in the plains of Yeriḥo.
And they ate of the produce of the land on the
morrow after the pessaḥ, matzot and parched
corn on the same day."

To answer the question of "when was the first pessaḥ" requires exploration into early origins in ethnology.

How Did Pessaḥ Originate?

One of the symbols of pessaḥ is the lamb.   Since a major means of livliehood for the ancient Hebrews was sheepherding, this means became a source of religious symbolization.   Some examples are offered: Among flock and herd-raising people, the sheep and bull were the main source of visible life, and the *form* through which the Deity sustained the people.   Thus, the god of the tribe was symbolized as the animal itself, for the gift of life is the god's own life.   If we understand this mental process, we can understand the incident of the Golden Calf, the national apostasy described in Exodus 32:1-35.[1]   Besides, one notes the strong suggestion of totemism in Numbers 2:2-31:   "The Israelites shall camp each with his standard, under the banners of their ancestral house..."   Although not elaborated upon, symbols and standards are mentioned repeatedly in reference to each individual tribe.   As was the ancient custom among diverse nations, an animal figure was the ensign designating a distinct military unit, the animal symbolizing the common possession by the group of the *spirit* of the animal.   Thus was kinship expressed, as well as fraternal responsibility.   Moreover, it is significant that the names of two matriarchs translate into animals: Raḥel means "ewe," and Leah means "wild cow."   As was noted elsewhere, the social structure and organization of these Aramean women was matriarchial, Yaacov (Jacob) living with his wives within the Akkadian-Hurrian legal category of *erebu*, that is, with the wife's clan.   This meant that all possessions belonged to the wife and her clan (Genesis 31:43).[2]

Another symbol of pessaḥ was the spring season.   At this season, there was a widespread sacrifice of the first fruits of crops and cattle.   Underlying this spring sacrifice was the idea that all first fruits were the special property of the Deity.   Two other ideas extend far back into the earliest human record, the idea of blood as both holy and as pollutant.

A sharp distinction came to be developed between divine and human life.   Blood was God's own property, hence, a tabu was placed upon it, extending even to animal life.   Blood had to be drained from an animal and poured out as a libation, to make it fit for consumption.   Being mysteriously close to divine life itself, blood possessed magical power, in addition to serving as the essential life-fluid of the animal. It was believed to have the power to arrest or stem the forward progress of a plague or disease. One may note some obscure passages in Exodus 4:24-26. At a night encampment on the return from Midian to Mitzrayim (Egypt) a "destroyer" encounters Moses and seeks to kill him.[3] His son, Gershom, born in Midian, was still uncircumcised. So, his wife, Zipporah, takes a flintsone and cuts off her son's foreskin, and touches Moses's legs with it saying: "You are truly a *hattan damim*, [or bridegroom of blood] to me." Moses is a bridegroom or *hattan*[4] cleansed by blood. Like all first-born, his son, Gershom, belongs to God, and his blood averts the design of the "destroyer." Later, it will be blood that will divert the tenth plague from slaying the first-born of the Hebrews.[5] Thus, by the time we come to the exodus of the Hebrews from bondage in Mitzrayim, there is already a full-blown tradition of a seasonal ceremony which receives a special interpretation in Exodus 12:21-27. Verse 21, 22 reads: "Kill the pessah," and apply some of the blood to the lintel. There is immediate comprehension of this injunction!

The Spring Festival (Textual Description)

There are some interesting instructions to Moses who – in his flight from Mitzrayim – sought refuge in Midian, where he is doing sheep herding for his father-in-law in the Wilderness of Sinai. He experiences a theophany at the Burning Bush and he is instructed to return to Mitzrayim on a special mission.

Exodus 3:18 relates: "And you shall say unto the King of Mitzrayim: ... let us go a distance of three days into the wilderness to sacrifice to YHWH our God." The request seems to be for a religious pilgrimage of three days only! In Exodus 5:1, the purpose for release is reiterated: "Let my people go that they may celebrate a festival for Me in the wilderness." Again there is mention of a known festival. This time, there is greater urgency. As recounted above, Moses himself had been accosted in Midian (Exodus 4:24-26) by a "destroyer" who wanted to slay him for not observing an important ritual. Thus, in Exodus 5:3, he seeks to convince The Paro[6] of the necessity for a three-day observance of the festival: "Let us go ... three days' journey into the wilderness to sacrifice to YHWH our God, lest He fall upon us with pestilence or the sword." Punishment is sure to overtake the people for its lapse in observance.

As is evident in these references to Moses in the Sinai Desert, and in his first appearances before the King of Mitzrayim, the pilgrimage is intended far in advance of the details of Exodus 12:1-12, 21-27[7]. In Exodus 12:14, the term "memorial" or remembrance (*zikaron*) is employed to indicate that the ancient spring festival is to be given a new interpretation.

The refusal by The Paro to recognize the urgency of the Hebrew pilgrimage brings the onset of the plagues, after which he begins to relent slowly but surely: "Remove the frogs and you can go and sacrifice" (Exodus 8:4). In Exodus 8:21 (after plague number four) he is acquiescent -- up to a point: "Go and sacrifice to your God *within* the land [of Mitzrayim]." To Moses's demurral, that the Mitzrians would be offended by the nature of the sacrifice, The Paro adds: sacrifice to your God, but do not go very far! (v. 24). Negotiations are continued in this vein. Before plague number eight, The Paro wants to know who it is that would be going on the pilgrimage (Exodus 10:8). Moses replies that it would be young and old, together with flocks and herds, because the festival *must* be observed. Yet, The Paro would agree only to the departure of the men alone (Exodus10:11). After the onset of the eighth plague, he relents and tells Moses to go with everybody – *except* the animals (Exodus 10:24-26). Moses explains that it is necessary to take along the animals since they do not know in advance what offerings are to be made, until their arrival at the site of their pilgrimage, outside the land. Finally, Exodus 11 announces the onset of the last plague (slaying of the first-born) from which the Hebrews are shielded, because they observe the traditional sacrifice on the soil of Mitzrayim itself. The injunction of Exodus 12:21 reads: "Pick out lambs for your families and kill the pessah." As was indicated earlier, this was understood at once, since it was a custom of long-standing.

The pessah was a rite observed at full moon in the month of Aviv. A lamb or goat was slaughtered at twilight and then eaten in the middle of the night, in commensality, with unleavened bread and bitter herbs. The eating was in haste to offset putrefecation, and left-over meat was burned before dawn. At the time of slaughter, a sponge-like plant, (the hyssop), was dipped in the victim's blood and sprinkled on the lintels of each hut. This was then followed by seven days of festival known as Matzot during which no fermented foods were to be eaten. In accordance with Exodus 12:1ff, a memorial was then established, marking this time-honored custom: "This month...

shall be the first of the months of the year for you." As may be seen, pessaḥ preceded the Exodus, otherwise it would be difficult to comprehend Moses's requests of The Paro to leave on a pilgrimage to observe the festival. Exodus 12:6-14 does not inaugurate a new ritual. It offers a new interpretation: "This day shall be to you one of remembrance."

The Fusion of Pessaḥ and Matzot

There is a common element in this festival: the re-weaving of the bonds of community at the beginning of a new season. This takes place through commensality and the absorption of a common substance (similar to the idea of turkey and cranberry sauce on Thanksgiving Day). Compacts and agreements were solemnized by breaking bread together, viz: Genesis 14:18-19 Avram and Malki-Zedek of Shalem; Genesis 21:27, Avraham and Avimelekh; Exodus 18:12, the sacrifical meal of Moses and Yithro. All these were examples of compact-making. (The modern day toast – "let's drink to that" – is a carry-forward of the ancient idea.)

The breaking of bread together had to do with the significance of food; i.e., it was looked upon as imparting new life and strength, therefore, it had to be prepared ritually, free of putrefaction arising from the process of fermentation itself. Thus, immediate consumption was a necessity to avert spoilage. To counteract the possibility of any impurity through putrefaction, strong herbs were eaten as condiments. After the consumption of the meal, participants in commensality were marked with a sign, indicating renewal of ties, by sprinkling blood on the forehead or on the lintels of huts. Since the Deity was also present at such a re-initiation rite, he would recognize the marking of those with whom a compact had been entered into.

The ancient Hebrews adapted this time-honored custom and related it to their own historic experience. Originally two distinct festivals, Pessaḥ and Matzot were combined and continually linked (See 2 Chronicles 35:17).[8] As Josephus declared: "The Feast of Unleavened bread succeeds that of the passover and falls on the fifteenth day of the month and continues seven days..." Since the Exodus from Mitzrayim coincided with the pessaḥ ritual, that ritual came to be connected with the tenth plague (the slaying of the first-born), while the unleavened dough was connected to the hurried departure from the land of slavery. Thus, the traditional ceremonials – older than the

Exodus itself – became a memorial *of* the Exodus. Pessaḥ survived until the Second Temple was destroyed, while Matzot continued unmodified, the memorial details being spelled out in Exodus 12:1-20, with verses 13,14 memorializing the passover aspect.

The Biblical Narrative as History

Rather than being a factual report, the biblical narrative of the Exodus is a saga, an epic, told and retold over generations, the beginning of the unification of discrete tribes that were to become confederated under a single banner: "Hear Israel, YHWH is our God, YHWH alone." It is significant that the declaration in the Hebrew is the singular form of the imperative: *Shema*, not *Shim'u*, the implication being one of unification (Israel), rather than disparate groups of Hebrews. Yet, this seems to suggest some later anachronistic treatment of prior events, i.e., a coordinated invasion of the land of Kenaan by a single unit, not its gradual conquest, in which there was an ultimate linkup of discrete tribal units pledged to unity under one divinity. The mere suggestion of discrete tribes of *Hebrews - not* Israel - each with its own totem divinity, has to be clouded over, if not suppressed, in the interest and dedication of a later age. But, in the process, an important understanding is sacrificed, i.e., why Mitzrian sources are silent about the Exodus. If, at the time, there was no distinct, unified nation of Yisrael, but a motley crowd of serfs on a reservation far away from Upper Egypt, the matter becomes clear.

Extra-biblical sources identify a special class of persons – not an ethnic unit – who were called Habiru or *Ivrim* (Hebrews).[9]   In the eighteenth pre-century, these were largely caravaneers, migrants, free-booters, mercenaries, and indentured servants, who did not enjoy landed civil rights. In the fourteenth century Amarna tablets, they are identified as raiders against towns in Amurru (Syria) and Retenu (or Kenaan). At Wadi Tumilat, the site of ancient Goshen, there was pasture ground reserved for such semi-nomadic groups under the Hekhos (Shepherd Kings) who controlled Mitzrayim for 200 years (ca. 1780-1570 BCE). When these foreign rulers were expelled by the Eighteenth Musurri Dynasty under Ahmose – who captured the former Hekhos (Hyksos) capital, Avaris, in the Nile Delta – Avaris was renovated and may have been renamed. Exodus 1: relates that the "children of Yisrael built the store cities of Pi-Thom[10] and Raamses. Raamses I[st] lived 400 years after the founding of Avaris in 1720 BCE, and a commemorative stele announced his observance of that 400th anniversary, namely, in 1320 BCE. This gives us some idea of the approximate period of Hebrew bondage. As was indicated earlier, Mitzrian sources do not refer to an exodus of a distinct national grouping; this is understandable, since the contingents of Hebrews who had been in Mitzrayim, were united more by common ancestry, rather than by a sense of national purpose.

Later Judaic development was to raise the exodus out of a context of ordinary chronicle; i.e., the events of the experience were to be viewed as transcending the time of their occurrence, embracing both memorial and re-enactment.[11] The exodus from a non-identity in serfdom to a national identification was intended as an experience in continuous liberation, whereby generations past, present, and future are linked in a sense of mission and destiny.

Afterword: From Pessah to Passover

The name Pessah (as well as Passover) is actually derived from a halting or skipping step in a "Lame Dance," associated with mourning ceremonies for a dead deity.   The usage, *Vayefasshu*, "And they danced [the skipping step in the Lame Dance] on the altar [of Baal]..." is to be found in the story of Eliyahu and his contest with the priests of Baal in 1 Kings 18:26.   The intensive form of the verb appears in verse 21: *poshim*, faltering or halting, while the consonants – whether in the noun or verb form – are identical: PSH.[12] The etymological origin connects the two names, which are here separated to indicate a difference in point of time and significance.   It should be emphasized that etymology is not to be mistaken for an Israelite ritual practice, but merely to indicate the origin of "skip-over" or pass-over as nomenclature.

The narrative of the Pessah of the Exodus (Exodus 12:1-27) – containing specifications and regulations of observance – is considered the original nucleus of the festival.   Yet, the very arrangement of the subsections in the Pentateuchal narrative represents an official tracing of the *gradual* ritual development of Passover.

It is significant that the Pessah sacrifice was never included in the various prophetic denunciations of animal sacrifice, for example, Jeremiah 7:22, where he says:
"... I did not command your ancestors concerning burnt offerings or sacrifices in the day I brought them out of the land of Mitzrayim."

The Pessah was unique in its grip on the Israelite mind as a communally redemptive sacrifice.

Notes

[1] The theology of the ancient Israelites was probably totemistic, i.e., the calf was the *form* through which YHWH made himself manifest. (There are those who say that the calf was the pedestal on which YHWH manifested himself.) Even in an advanced age, e.g., the twentieth century, some theological conceptions project God in human *form*.

[2] Genesis 31:43: "Then Lavan said to Yaacov. 'The daughters are my daughters, the children are my children, and the flocks are my flocks; all that you see is mine.' "

Genesis 31:19, 32-35, recounts an incident of theft, by Rahel, of *Teraphim* (images) belonging to her father, Lavan. In a cuneiform document from Nuzi in Mesopotamia in the 15th pre-century, we learn that to claim an estate required possession of the household god, which was legally the deed to the property. Thus, by her action, Rahel was trying to secure title for her husband, Yaacov, (which made Lavan most unhappy).

[3] Mitzrayim: The biblical name is preferred to the much later version, Egypt. A resident of Mitzrayim is termed a Mitzrian, (Musuri in Akkadian).

[4] *Hattana*, in Arabic, derives from a verbal root meaning "to circumcise."

[5] The connection between the slaying of the *pessah* and the first-born males is found in Exodus 13:15: "Therefore, I sacrifice to YHWH every first male issue of the womb, but redeem every first-born among my sons." (The rite of redemption of first-born sons (*pidyon haben*) is referred to in the Book of Numbers 3:13.)

[6] *The* Paro (or Per'o), ruler of Mitzrayim, is similar to the title, *The* Tsar or *The* Kaiser. Literally, Per'o refers to the House (of divinity).

[7] Exodus 12:12: "For that night I will go through the land of Mitzrayim and strike down every first-born in the land..."

[8] The Chronicles text is a re-statement of an original version in 2 Kings 23:21-23: "And the king commanded all the people saying: 'Keep the pessah unto YHWH, your God...' For there was not kept such a pessah from the days of the judges... nor in all the days of the kings of Yisrael nor of the kings of Yehudah, but in the eighteenth year of King Yoshiyahu was this pessah kept to YHWH in Yerushalayim." (A slight difference is noted, this version referring to the "days of the judges...")

[9] *Apiru, Abiru, Ivri* are variants. The designation referred more to a vocation of stateless people: caravaneers or donkey-drivers.

[10] Probably Per-Atum (the House of Atum), in the language of Mitzrayim.

[11] The patriarchial past was linked with the then-present, i.e., the generation in Mitzrayim. The future was then united with both of these.

[12] The consonants PSH are the same for the term *Piseah* (Lame One, or lameness). See Leviticus 21:18 and Deuteronomy 15:21 for the usage.

6. *The Ten Lost Tribes Were Not Lost*

Introduction

The story of the mysterious disappearance of the Ten Tribes of Israel is a fanciful one, resting on an appealing belief of a homogeneous, land-locked people confined to a single country, who were cast into national exile as a consequence of sinfulness. The consequent hunt for "lost tribes" was largely the result of Western misunderstanding of biblical passages, and the substitution of imaginative construction in place of studied explanation. Isra-elite tribes never disappeared as imagined in the poetic phrase "lost ten tribes"; they did, however, lose their discrete identities when melding, amalgamation, and national unity occurred under a more or less long-term process of mo-narchical centralization. The phrase makes its appeal perhaps because of its tonal resonance, yet it is but a superficial captioning of a sparse number of facts. What had been "lost" was not a people, but a chapter of its history.

The Ten Tribe Unit

The notion of ten tribes as a cohesive unit is a throwback in time probably to the patriarchial days of Yaacov (Jacob) himself, and the listing of his twelve sons as comprising the body of Israel. A similar imaginative construction is the invasion of Kenaan as a unitary body under Yehoshua (Joshua); it makes for neatness, convenience, and orderliness in thought, but it hardly corre-sponds to fact: gradual infiltration and conquest of the land.

Very early in Israelite history, the tribe of Shimon (Simeon) was absorbed by Yehudah (Judah) and its neighbors, and by the time of the Davidic/ Solomonic monarchy, Yehudah and Binyamin (Judah and Benjamin) had been largely amalgamated. From earliest times, the house of Levi had been dif-fused, occupying no distinct area or district within the land of Kenaan. Then, too, the trans-Jordanian tribes of Reuven, Gad, and half of Manasseh (i.e., Gilead) were disposed towards amalgamation as a geographic unit, to avert dispersal; even though the Reubenites merged with Manassites, they moved ever eastwards, ultimately to be replaced by Moabites, while the Gaddites drifted southeastwards, ultimately settling in Arabia. Thus, the tally of ten distinct tribes is clearly a miscalculation, one of blurring and overstatement: Shimon, Gad, Reuven, and Manasseh cannot be regarded as persevering and pure entities. In this sense, they become "lost" through diffusion and amalgamation.

The idea of a ten tribe composite unit is poetic, but it is probably connected to some incidents recorded in 1 Samuel 8:4 and 1 Kings 11:31. In the former, all the elders or clan heads of various tribes importune the seer, Shemuel (Samuel), for a king and, subsequently, a representative from the tribe of Binyamim (Benjamin) is chosen (1 Samuel 10:20-24). In 2 Samuel 19:44, which records the restoration of David to his throne following an unsuccessful revolt, we encounter the following assertion: "And the men of Israel answered the men of Judah and said: 'We have ten parts in the king... [ten votes].'"[1] (This, of course, refers to the ruling class whose vote – as a body – in the national council, can crown a king.) What is significant in the assertion of "ten parts" is that it occurs well before the division of Israel into two separate kingdoms. When the fragile unity of Israel is later split in two, the text of 1 Kings 11:31-32 relates that the secessionist, Yeravam (Jeroboam) is to receive "ten pieces" and Reḥavam [David's grandson] one tribe or *shevet*.[2] Does this mark the origin of the ten tribe unit expression? Given the uncertainty of the precise number of unit votes of the tribes in a national council, the idea of a ten tribe unit appears rather to reflect the tendentious anachronistic interpretations of a later day, as suggested below.

Although the expression "ten lost tribes" occurs only within the context of the deportations by the kingdom of Asshur in the eighth century BCE, there is something very curious in the textual accounts of the event, appearing some centuries later as 2 Kings 17:6, 18:11, and 15:29. Nowhere, in these major references to the deportations, does the term tribe (*shevet*, or the plural *shevatim*) appear! Is it because the term for tribe (shevet) also has the meaning of "staff" as in an officer's baton or the sceptre of a ruler, such usage appearing widely, in Genesis 38:18, Judges 5:14, and Isaiah 10:5 and 14:5? (See Note 12.) This explanation does not satisfy as will be indicated shortly. The text in 2 Kings 18:11 makes no references to *tribe*(s) but reads simply: "And the king of Asshur carried Israel away unto Asshur..." Was this written by persons who, themselves, were no longer part of identifiable tribal structures? One other avenue has to be explored.

The usage "Israel" – as well as the expansive "all Israel" – appears in 2 Samuel 17:10, 11, 14, and 19:42 (as well as in Kings), these latter references describing the revolt of Prince Avshalom (Absalom) against his father, King

David, and the crushing of that uprising. The setting in which the expression "all Israel" occurs makes it clear that only the official military aristocracy or dominant social elements were involved. That the very term itself, *Israel*, refers to the ruling class is made explicit in 1 Kings 9:22. Here, the relationship between King Shelomoh and Israel is described: "... they were the men of war, and his [Solomon's] servants, and his princes and his captains, and commanders of his chariots." Surely, the passages in 2 Kings 17:6 and 18:11, regarding the deportation of *Israel* to Assyria, refer only to the ruling class. That a class represents the entire nation is reflected in the manner of expression which regards a dominant group (or section) as a whole. Thus, Judah – dominant in the south – was often taken as the nation,[3] as was Ephrayim – dominant in the north – looked upon as *Israel*, almost uniformly by the prophets.[4] Certainly, Ephrayim's rejection of the Davidic dynasty was expressed in the name of the entire nation: "To your tents, Israel; now see to your own house David." (1 Kings 12:16.)

To retrace now to the matter of a composite ten tribe unit, it appears as embedded in narratives regarding the restoration of David to his throne after the rebellion of Avshalom (Absalom), and in the later subsequent split of the unity of Israel into two kingdoms, at the accession to the throne of David's grandson, Reḥavam (933 BCE). By the time of the destruction of the northern kingdom of Israel and the deportation of its aristocracy by the Kingdom of Assyria some two centuries later, there had developed an interpretive (largely poetic) anachronism regarding a ten tribe unit, even though the whereabouts of at least two of the "parts" or "pieces" (i.e., Simeon and Levi) was problematic. A simpler hypothesis may also suffice: the written documents (the Books of Kings) are post-exilic products of the 5th century BCE; i.e., the tribal structure had been completely erased and the residue of the nation had been fused. Thus, the writers spoke in then-contemporary perspectives: "... the king of Asshur took Samaria, and carried *Israel* away unto Asshur..."

The Assyrian Deportations

In the accounts of the Assyrian conquest of the kingdom of Israel, two references to the Sargonid deportation of 721 BCE are similar in their recording, 2 Kings 17:6 and 18:11: "And the King of Asshur carried Israel away unto Asshur..." The deportation was mainly from the plains of Ephrayim, that tribe, as indicated, constituting the official leadership of the northern kingdom. There was, however, an earlier deportation (733-32 BCE) under Tiglath Pilesser III, recorded in 2 Kings 15:29. Here, the text reports that the deportations were from Gilead in trans-Jordan and from the territory of the tribe of Naphtali in Galilee. A rather curious summary statement appears in the Book of 1 Chronicles 5:26, to the effect that the deportation in 733-32 BCE under "Pul[u]" or "Tillegath Pilnesser" [sic] involved only the trans-Jordanian tribes of Reuven, Gad, and half of Manasseh. The scale of the deportation is not given, nor is the conflict between the two records of the event in 2 Kings and 1 Chronicles resolved. Fortunately, Assyrian records provide some indication of the size of these deportations; in turn, such information sheds light on the larger question of whether the tribes were "lost." It must be remembered that in a global age, there is a tendency to conceive of wars as involving hundreds of thousands because the reference point is, in fact, global. However, in ancient wars, the numbers involved were far fewer; in many cases, only city-states were involved, not continental powers. Then, too, one has to allow for the tendency of victorious rulers to employ hyperbole in referring to their exploits; particularly when inscribed on state-sponsored tablets, figures tend to be over-stated rather than under-reported.

The scale of the Assyrian deportations may well be contrasted with some figures given in the Pentateuch. The Book of Numbers 31:35 details what the loser could expect in a war; the narrative reports 32,000 Midianite maidens as captives, (reflecting the widespread practice that war meant exile and slavery for many). However, it may be noted that this number of captives from Israel's conquest of the trans-Jordan area was larger than the total number that Sharrukin II (Sargon IInd) of Assyria claims to have deported from the Samarian capital in 721 BCE. The official goverment inscription indicates that 27,290 of Samaria's inhabitants were taken away, that fifty chariots were collected from them, and that a governor was placed over the remainder, who were allowed allowed to keep their property.[5]

As mentioned heretofore, the text of 2 Kings 17:6 (and 18:11) does not state that ten tribes were carried off; the reference is to "Israel" as a collective. How does one interpret that usage? It might be thought that this included the whole populace, but the references to 2 Samuel 19:42 and 1 Kings 9:22 are recalled here; i.e.,"Israel" means the ruling class or dominant social elements. The pride of an aristocracy cultivates the notion that *it* is synonymous with the nation as a whole. For instance, the remark attributed to Louis

XIV that he was, in effect, the State, was less one of arrogance and more ingenuous and to the point; it simply described the reality. Similarly, if one reads of Napoleon's war on Russia, there is no difficulty in understanding that France, as a nation, is being summed up in his name. To underscore the matter of usage, a passage relating to the reign of King Ḥizkiyahu (720-692 BCE), appearing in 2 Chronicles 30:1-27, clarifies what 2 Kings 18:11 intends by the phrase "And the King of Asshur carried Israel away unto Asshur...": It cannot be inferred that all Israel went into exile at the time of the fall of Samaria. (See Note 6.)

As indicated above, there was an earlier deportation – prior to the fall of Samaria – under Pulu or Tiglath Pilesser III of Assyria, in 733-32 BCE. Parts of his victory inscription read: "30,000 I carried off from their cities and placed them in the province of the city of ...1233 people I settled in the province of the land of Ulluba."[7]   The numbers recorded in the deportations of Tiglath Pilesser III and Sargon II may be contrasted with Sennacherib's invasion of the Kingdom of Judah (ca. 699 BCE) twenty-two years after the conquest of the northern Kingdom of Israel. 200,150 exiles were numbered from southwestern Judah[8]; this is eight times as many as Sargon deported from the Kingdom of Israel! One hundred years later, the raid of Nebuchadrezzar into Judah in 597 BCE resulted in a large scale deportation into Babylon, including the royal family itself. Even allowing for exaggeration of exploits by the conquerors (Sennacherib of Assyria and Nebuchadrezzar of Babylon) in their respective state-sponsored inscriptions, the deportation by Sargon II seems small by comparison; it would suggest that one has to look elsewhere to account for "lost ten tribes."

Indeed, the widely dispersed Jews – as detailed in Isaiah 11:11,12: "... from Asshur and from Mitzrayim, and from Pathros, and Cush, and Elam and Shinar, and from Hamath and from the islands of the sea..." – could not possibly be the result of deportations by Tiglath Pilesser and Sargon. Even though Asshur is named as one of the places of dispersal, these deportees were but a small fraction of the total number of Jews residing outside the land of Israel. For instance, there certainly was settlement in Mitzrayim (Egypt) during the reign of Shelomoh (Solomon) (973-33 BCE), given the marriage of state between him and the Egyptian princess. Then, too, commerce with, and migration to, some distant places was a consequence of the close connection between Israel and the maritime Phenecians who reached and settled

Carthage (Qarta Ḥadash/Qarthash-New City) in mid-ninth century BCE. At the same time, during the ninth century BCE, seventy years of ongoing war with neighboring Aram reduced the northern kingdom of Israel seriously, even as it involved dispersal into Aramean territory and ethnic inter-mingling between Aram and Israel. For instance, in 2 Kings 13:7, it is noted that King Yehoahaz (816-800 BCE) – after continuous warfare with Aram throughout the seventeen years of his reign – was left with but 10,000 foot soldiers, 50 horses, and ten chariots.

Israel Not Confined to a Single Country

The usual internal picture of Israel is that of a people gathered within one country. It is hard to imagine that Israelite settlement *outside* the land of Kenaan *preceded,* or was contemporaneous with, its settlement in Kenaan itself. As a matter of record, Israel was in North Africa, Egypt, and Abyssinia almost from the very beginning of its history. As early as the period of the Judges (1400-1000 BCE), if not earlier, one may see the diffusion of Israel in the documentary reference to Danites dwelling in ships, with Asherites on the seashore (Judge 5:17). This may be taken as an apparent indication of commercial activity abroad and eventual colonial activity in North Africa. Subsequent Israelite settlement entered Transjordania, Arabia, Egypt, East Africa, Asia Minor, and the Black Sea area – much of such settlement preceding the national dispersions of the eighth pre-century. In addition, the ideological or religious influence of Israel was a major export product of no small consequence. In the centuries before the rise of Christianity and Islam, it was Yahu-ism[9] that spread far and wide, with adaptations on the local level. For instance, an active Egyptian-Jewish community extended as far back as the seventh or eighth pre-century, and while Jewish settlers in Asia Minor and southeastern Europe had a much briefer local history, nevertheless such Jewries as those in Syria, Armenia, the Eastern Mediterranean islands and the Balkans, as well as those in greater Carthage and Italy, consisted of former proselytes and their descendants.[10] One can hardly consider such ideological diffusion a "loss," albeit that it may represent a dilution of the Yahu-ism expressed within the land of Israel proper.

Deportees as Colonists

The image of exiles and deportees is usually drawn from a later age, e.g., from vague impressions of Rome and Egypt, of galley slaves and work in mines. While the lot of the vanquished in ancient wars was not enviable, a picture of uniform misery is too easily fabricated. In 2 Kings 17:24-28, one reads of respect by the Assyrian conqueror for the god of the land of Israel, through his provision for the religious instruction of the local populace. Asshur also maintained a land exchange system, including asylum land, the product of a long history, reflecting practices elsewhere. For instance, ancient Egypt would invite into its borders herders, and would provide them with acreage, whole ethnic groups often being viewed as farmers and traders or even colonists. In the ancient world, the accompaniment of a war involved not only mass migration but included the importation of colonists considered desirable because of a particular skill or trade,[11] or in order to settle a sparsely populated area. Thus, when Asshur mounted its assault against the southern kingdom of Judah (699 BCE), the Assyrian emissary (Rav-shakeh) offered a piece of land in Asshur to those Judahites who would desert their king, Ḥizkiyahu (2 Kings 18:32). How can such an offer be explained in the light of popular images? Even deportations were not synonymous with slavery. The prophet Yirmiyahu's message to the deportees to Babylon is instructive: "Seek the peace of the city whither I have caused you to be carried away captive. Build ye houses and dwell in them." (Jeremiah 29:4-7).

Here, mention must also be made of an ancient social institution: the employment of conquered people in the service of the conqueror (found in Hittite records of the fourteenth pre-century as well as Assyrian records of the 13th pre-century). A conqueror on the march would receive into his service those subjugated by war or by treaty; thus, cities would make terms with the conqueror, hoping to recoup their losses by pillage of the next cities on the line of march. The Gibeonites in Kenaan (Joshua 9:3ff) offer a striking example of treaty-making obeisance in order to avoid military conquest. "We are your servants," the Gibeonites declare; "and now make ye a covenant with us." (Joshua 9:8,11).

Another institution, that of the *zakku* or *zakkutu* is to be noted. The *zakku* represented a class of foreigners who were used as frontier guards or police. A description of the institution is found in 2 Samuel 15:18, 19, where King

David's royal bodyguard is composed of Kerethites (C'retim/Cretans), Pelethites (Peletim) and Gittites, under the command of Ittai, the Gittite (i.e., from Gath in Philistia). In later general history, one reads of the Roman use of Germans as personal bodyguards for the Emperors Tiberius and Caligula; still later, the employment of Mamelukes in Egypt and Janissaries in the Ottoman Empire, and the Papal use of Swiss Guards. In all these cases, the guards would swear personal fealty, the service of their swords, to their Master. The Western medieval tradition of the knight's oath or absolute service to his master is well-known and well-documented, and reflects the nature of the corresponding *zakku* service in the Near East.

The *zakku* institution of soldier-colonies and shrine guards is, then, an ancient one, and helped to develop the colonial aspect of Yahu-ism, which explains such Jewish soldier-outposts as the Elephantine military colony at Aswan in Egypt. Thus, in the Assyrian deportations of the eighth pre-century, there was less danger of total assimilation of Jewish subjects than is generally imagined. Indeed, communication between Jerusalem and the centers of exile in Asshur and Bavel (Babylon) was maintained. Jeremiah 51:31 tells of a communication system between Jerusalem and Babylon in the form of courier posts in close connection. Ezekiel 33:21 and Nehemiah 1:2 clearly indicate courier posts in operation, the system being continued under Persian rule, as recounted in the books of Ezra and Nehemiah, in which the position of record-keepers also is portrayed. (See Ezra 4:7-13.)

The Picture of a Restoration to Glory

Enough has been said about the diffusion of the people of Israel and its ideas to indicate that it was not a one-time phenomenon, the result of a single major dispersal. Nevertheless, there *was* a national trauma occurring in 721 BCE, with the destruction of the northern kingdom of Israel. This, in turn, brought forth a theodicy, the justification of the tragedy as well as visions of a future redemption.[12] The vision of Isaiah 27:13, on general restoration, has been adapted into the liturgy, helping to fashion and perpetuate the "lost tribes" theory: "And it shall be on that day when the Great Shofar is sounded that those who were lost in the land of Asshur and those banished in the land of Mitzrayim shall come and bow down unto YHWH in the holy mountain at Yerushalayim." (One notes that this is a proclamation of religious homage, not an historical description.)

The foregoing reference is clearly a message of hope to a people who had just experienced conquest and the massive loss of ancestral land. As incorporated into the liturgy, the verse announces the return of deportees who had been transported abroad. In another section, in an usual display of word-painting, the prophet describes how both the kingdoms of Israel and Judah would fall before Asshur which, then, itself, will be swept away. (See Isaiah 10:5, 6, 10-13, 20, 21.) In the grand vision of chapter 11, Yishayahu declares in verses 11, 12 that "God will... recover the remnant of his people who remain from Asshur, and from Mitzrayim, and from Pathros, and Cush, and Elam and Shinar, and from Hamath and from the islands of the sea... and He will gather together the scattered of Judah from the four corners of the earth."

One notes the diffusion of Israel – not a deportation – to such places as Elam and Shinar (on the Persian gulf) and to the islands of the Sea (how far west in the Mediterranean one may conjecture). What is significant in this reference is that the restoration of Israel is general; it is not only of those deported from the northern kingdom or the southern kingdom; there is a return to Zion of *all* Israel - a national re-unification.

The writings of Yishayahu, Yirmiyahu, Yehezkel, and the late prophet Zekhariah are unanimous in picturing a *single* restoration. Yirmiyahu's vision is particularly striking. In his description of a return from *general* dispersal (Jeremiah 16:14, 15), it is presented as actually outranking the escape from Egyptian bondage in national importance, to wit: "... no more shall it be said: 'as YHWH lives, who brought the children of Israel up out of Mitzrayim' but rather, 'as YHWH lives, who brought the children of Israel up from the northern land, and from all the lands to which he had expelled them'; and will bring them back into the land which I gave to their ancestors." (The same words are expressed again in Jeremiah 23:7,8.) The point is that restoration refers to a re-unification of a people sundered by its own wilfulness and desires, as well as its enforced dispersal by a conqueror.

In the Aliyah to Zion (or restoration) from Babylonian Exile, authorized under Kurush (Cyrus) the Mede in 537 BCE, the picture of the return includes Josephites, along with the expellees from the Kingdom of Judah. Jerusalem is to be the center of a re-united people, Ephrayimites (Josephites) sharing in the diminutive - but restored - state. The two peoples of Israel and

Judah (Josephites and Judahites) are united in prophetic thought, and it stretches interpretation to believe that Judah alone was restored, while the restoration of Joseph never occurred and – if one follows the popular theory of tribes that were "lost" permanently – never will. Zechariah 8:13 makes clear the nature of the Restoration: "As you were a curse among the nations, O House of Judah and House of Israel, so will I save you and ye shall be a blessing." Further in 10:6, Zechariah declares: "And I will strengthen the House of Judah and will save the House of Joseph and I will bring them again to the places ... and they shall be as though I had not cast them off."

Summary

1. The ten tribe unit associated with the northern kingdom of Israel was, at most, an eight tribe unit, excluding the tribes of Simeon and Levi. It is also doubtful whether tribal strucures were preserved intact in the face of fusion and amalgamation between such tribes as Ephrayimites and Manassites, Reubenites and Manassites, Judahites and Benjaminites.

2. From the very beginning of its national history, Israel was neither a single, homogeneous, nor contiguous unit; its contingents being located in Egypt, Abyssinia and North Africa. At these locations, there were propagandists for a primitive form of Yahu-ism.

3. From the time of the entry of Israel into Kenaan to the destruction of both northern and southern political entities by Assyria and Babylonia, there had been commercial and colonial activity beyond the geographical confines of the territory of Israel. The reference to Jewries to be reassembled from the islands of the sea and "from the four corners of the earth" (Isaiah 11:11, 12) cannot otherwise be adequately explained.

4. Despite the loss of a major war by Israel in the eighth pre-century, there was not a sudden dispersal but – as indicated in the proceeding – a gradual diffusion. Moreover, the deportation to Assyrian territory was less of a loss and more the transport of Yahu-ism to lands of the East. As Josephus had observed in the first century C.E., there were two Israels: one in Judea and one in the East in Assyria, Babylonia, and Persia. This division was a result of the conquest of the homeland, with large numbers of Jews remaining permanently in the country of the conqueror or liberator – as in the case of

Persia.

5. The theory of the "Lost Ten Tribes," is inferred from the vision of restoration in Isaiah 27:13, that vision – later incorporated into the liturgy – was expanded upon in romance and fancy, in non-Jewish as well as Jewish, literary treatment.

6. The theodicy implicit in the fabric of the lost tribes theory accounts for a national disaster as the consequence of violation of covenantal obligations. Exile was the price of sinfulness,[13] but ultimately, there would be a general re-unification of the nation, and the land would be restored as a central sanctuary by divine decree.

Notes

[1] This would mean that Simeonite and Levite clans still retained a vote in the national council or plenum even though, in actuality, Simeon had amalgamated with Judah and Levites were diffused within the body of the nation as a whole. It also would indicate that despite the fusion of Judah and Benjamin (see 1 Kings 11:32) and Manasseh and Ephrayim, each tribe retained a separate vote in the national council. At best, this kind of calculation does not reflect the reality of an eight tribe unit.

[2] The statement in 1 Kings 11:31-32, that David is to receive one *shevet* or tribe, makes it very clear that Benjamin had been absorbed into Judah. How the reckoning of ten tribes is arrived at, is very far from clear!

[3] There are some naive students of biblical history who interpret a narrative as a biography of an individual life, such as Judah. In particular, the name is the eponym of a collectivity of Judahites.

[4] Hosea 6:4: "What shall I do to you Ephrayim? What shall I do to you Judah?"
Isaiah 28:1:"Woe to the crown of arrogance [worn by] of the drunkards of Ephrayim."
Jeremiah 31:20: "Is Ephrayim my precious child?"
Zechariah 10:6:"And I will strengthen the House of Judah and will save the House of Joseph..."

[5] "Sargon II (721-705 BCE): The Fall of Samaria," in James B. Pritchard, *The Ancient Near East, An Anthology of Texts and Pictures*. Princeton University Press, 1969, p.195.

[6] 2 Chronicles 30:1-27 relates how Ḥizkiyahu, king of Judah, wrote letters to Ephrayim and Manasseh to observe the Passover (*after* the destruction of the northern kingdom):
"So the posts went with the letters from the king... throughout all Israel and Judah ... saying: 'Ye children of Israel, turn back to YHWH... that He may return to the remnant that are escaped of you out of the hand of the kings of Asshur.' " (2 Chronicles 30:6)
Verse 10: "So the posts passed from city to city through the country of Ephrayim and Manasseh, even unto Zevulun ... Nevertheless men of Asher and Manasseh and of Zevulun humbled themselves and came to Jerusalem." [See verse 18, where men of Yissachar are also mentioned.]

The passage seems to reflect the political considerations of the period, i.e., the central sanctuary in Jerusalem was respected by the residents of the north as well as the south. Just shortly after the destruction of Samaria in 721 BCE, the people of the north transferred their loyalties to the sanctuary at Jerusalem. The passage sheds light on the extent of the exile of northern Israel.

[6] The account of a special celebration of Passover under Ḥizkiyahu contained in the passage is, however, questionable in point of historicity, i.e., with regard to the manner of ritual observance. This is a special subject unto itself and cannot be detailed here, except to say that the writer is probably describing the usages of his own day (ca. 400-250 BCE) rather than the eighth century BCE. Moreover, the conflict between 2 Chronicles 30:1-27 and 2 Kings 23:21-23 (referring to King Yoshiyahu) is glaring.

[7] *Ancient Records of Assyria and Babylonia* (Daniel David Luckenbill), Volume I, 770, 1926-27. Cited in Jack Finegan, *Light From the Ancient Past,* Priceton University Press, 1949, p. 174.

[8] "Sennacherib (704-681 BCE): The Siege of Jerusalem," Pritchard, *op. cit.*, p. 200.

[9] Judaism is a much later flower than Yahu-ism. The latter term is preferred, to highlight the life and death struggle the prophets waged in order to ensure that Yahu was to be recognized by the entire nation of Israel.

[10] According to some estimates, before the fall of Jerusalem in 70 CE., about three million Jews lived in an area extending on a line from Crete to Armenia alone. Some of this population were refugees from Maccabean wars, Herodian wars, Parthian raids, perennial clashes between Syria and Judea, Roman conquests, and the post 70 CE large scale Jewish uprisings in the Roman colonial possessions of Cyrenaica in North Africa and in Armenia.

[11] For instance, in *Antiquities of the Jews* X, 11:1, Josephus states that the captives of Nebuchadnezzar II (in the sixth century BCE) were Jews, Phoenecians, Syrians, and various Egyptians who were to be "placed as *colonies* in the most proper places of Babylonia." This kind of testimony - offhand, as one might say - is most revealing!

[12] The prophetic refrain regarding the destruction of both kingdoms, southern as well as northern, sees it as the instrumentality of divine correction. The theodicy is clearly expressed in Isaiah 10:5: "O Asshur, rod of my anger [shevet api], into whose hand I have placed the staff of my indignation, I send him [Asshur] against an ungodly nation."
[One may note here the alternate usage of the term *shevet.*] Another stark example of the refrain is found in Ezekiel 23. The entire chapter of forty-nine verses is an indictment and condemnation of the "lewd sisters," Samaria and Jerusalem who, in their promiscuous harlotry and idolatry, have to be taught a harsh lesson. A milder form of the refrain is set forth in Jeremiah 29:4: "... to all the Exile whom I [God] have caused to be carried away captive, from Jerusalem to Babylon": See also Jeremiah 31:18: "I have heard Ephrayim bemoaning: 'You have chastised me and I was chastised.' "

[13] Given the widespread acceptance of the theodicy [See references in preceding note] and its penetration into the folk-consciousness itself, a tradition of historicity was euhemerized through later generations of Bible-readers, non-Jewish and Jewish alike. In Jewish liturgical worship, threnodies - many composed in medieval Spain and chanted on the Ninth of Av (the date which commemorates national disasters) - express the very theme: Exile was the consequence of Israel's sins.

7. *Transcending Religious Barriers:*
The Many Faces of God

Prefatory Note

This lecture was presented at the Theodor Herzl Institute following the author's return from a stay as Fulbright Scholar in Korea. It was first delivered as part of a symposium to the Seoul International Women's Association, at the Hyatt Hotel in Seoul, Korea, on October 24, 1989. The somewhat tendentious sub-title was given to representatives of Roman Catholicism, Protestantism, Islam, Buddhism, and Judaism, and respondents were asked to frame their presentation under the following structural outline:

1. What makes your religion unique from others,
   i.e., essential beliefs and the image it projects of God?
2. What does it share in common with other religions?
3. What can the [Judaic] faith learn from other religions?

At the outset, it may be observed that the content of the lecture is distinct from the others presented in this collection, both in substance and form. The subject matter is pointedly theological and its purpose was – as the title reveals – to consider how religious barriers could be transcended, especially since God has many faces or, at least, is *viewed* as possessing many faces. (This tendentious pre-supposition will be examined in the response.)

* * * * * * * * * * * *

1. What makes your religion unique from others, i.e., essential beliefs and the image it projects of God?

In the year 63 BCE, Pompey and his Roman legions entered Jerusalem. He came to the inner sanctum of the Temple, called the Holy of Holies, to discover the nature of the God who dwelt there. All that was known of this God was the ineffableness of his name, a tetragrammaton of four letters: YHWH (later to become badly corrupted into "Jehovah" in pronunciation, and inadequately translated into "The Lord"). The Roman soldiers were advised that YHWH was invisible and that even the letters signifying his existence were unpronounceable, thus indicative of his indiscoverable nature; so they poked the air with their spears as they entered the Temple's inner courts. Pompey found nothing but empty space in the Holy of Holies, whereupon he declared that Judeans were atheists, because they believed in nothing that could be apprehended by the senses. To Pompey - as to many others before and since - God had to have substance, form and shape.

Thus, the response to the question is a simple one. To borrow a peculiarly twentieth century expression, the "image" that Judaic thought projects of God is *none*; therein lies its uniqueness and originality. Judaic thought rejects *any* portrayal of the divine as the highest sacrilege. Roman attempts in the first century of the Common Era to transport images – whether of eagles or emperors – into the city of Jerusalem were met with the most determined opposition, even to the point of martyrdom. God looks like nothing we have ever seen; how, then, is it possible to construct a mental image of his being-ness? Not only are we unable to form a picture of God, we are unable to give expression to that essence in words. But when we do speak and make references to a divine existence, the words are only approximations, and do not intend to convey what is meant in ordinary discourse. When terms such as "He" and "Him" are, perforce, employed, they are, in themselves, devoid of gender implications, for God has no sexuality. To conceptualize gender because in the usual case, "he" implies masculinity would, in the unique context of deity, be akin to idol construction, albeit the idol is composed of verbal constructs that have been objectified, through human reification of grammar.

Furthermore, to speak of the "many faces of God" in a literal sense, would likewise be the ultimate in anthropomorphization: the ascription of human qualities to the divine. God is made to look like us! I remember very well some posters and handbills at my college (CCNY) that complained of a "white" god; a black "image" was demanded, in order for people of color to be able to "relate" to the divinity. Such blatantly projective anthropomorphism would again be regarded as idolatrous: a construction of God that would reflect a human visage and human characterisics!

To be sure, the expression "many faces of God" can be used in a figurative sense as metaphor. However, this would seem to imply a promiscuous polytheism. Between anthropomorphism and polytheism there is not much to choose. In contradistinction, Judaic thought has tended towards an absolutism - the defining characteristic of a mature monotheism. That is to say, there are *no* other gods. Moreover, even God's oneness is unique; it is not one amongst many, but sole - alone. Nor is it a oneness composed of a plurality of substances, as in pantheism.

While Judaic thought cannot say what God *is*, it does say what God is *not*. To respond to the query "what makes the religion unique," its originality lies precisely in its negative theology,. God has *no* image, *no* face, *no* sex, *no* shape, *no* form, *no* plurality. As stated earlier, even the *one-ness* of God, itself, has no definability apart from absolute uniqueness, soleness, aloneness.

To point out that the subject matter of theology – as a distinct discipline of study – is a late entrant into the main Judaic body of thought, may aid in the comprehension of the foregoing ideas. Indeed, it is very difficult to speak of *Judaism* as a fixed doctrine, rather than as an evolving belief system. Even when core beliefs are identified – one God as Creator of the universe – one has to stop short: the *nature* of the divine is not specified nor specifiable.

2. What does the religion share in common with other religions?

Despite the inability to say what God is – which, for some, may be an unattractive and even repelling feature – Judaic thought, nevertheless, asserts that a Creator exists. God is. This "is-ness," being-ness" or - in the Hebraic idiom - "I am-ness" constitutes reality. As Kant would inform us: an idea is in no way an image, even though it is real; its metaphysical function is regulative; it serves as a guiding concept. The "I am-ness" of the Judaic God-concept functions regulatively. In this regard, the absence of the present tense of the verb *to be* within the system of Hebrew grammar is striking and arresting. While one can express the past (I was), or the future (I will be), there is no way to express "I am" or "I exist." One simply refers to life in general to indicate that one lives: "I breathe," or I "inhale," are possible, but "I am" is not. This says something about the concept of *the real* as being synonymous with divine being-ness.

In addition to asserting that God *is,* Judaic thought denies that *chance* accounts for the existence of a universe. This would seem to be implicit in the concept of divinity as reality; God's "is-ness" is a negation of happenstance and accident. The universe was called into being by the presence of a divine Creator, that presence being the fiat of creation itself. The liturgy contains such expressions as "Master of the Universe" which indicate that disorder and chaos are *daily* held at bay by command (i.e., the existence or reality) of the Creator.

Yet, order is not confined only to the physical sphere; it involves the introduction of the principle of equity and justice into the human world. The Psalmist describes it poetically: "The heavens rejoice and the earth is glad, the sea resounds, the fields are jubilant, the trees of the forest sing for joy before YHWH, for he comes as judge of the earth, in righteousness and e-quity." (Psalm 96:11-13) Disorder and lawlessness in the moral, i.e., inter-human, world are dispelled through the reality of God's existence; righteous-ness and justice in human dealings constituting a consequence of that exist-ence.

A characteristic shared by many faith systems lies in the conceptualization of a deity anthropomorphically, as seen in our linguistic expressions. We tend to refer to God as having emotions and we project human behavior onto the deity. Sometimes, this is a result of too literal an interpretation of Scrip-tural pasages. Careful reflection permits us to comprehend that, anthropo-morphic expressions notwithstanding, such characterizations are not to be taken as accurate descriptions; rather, they represent the inadequacy and limi-tations of human language and thought itself.

3. What can the Judaic faith learn from other religions?

The principle of divine revelation seems to underlie many faith systems, thereby creating a warrant for their very being. Indeed, the human ability to know – itself – is seen as emanating from divine inspiration and blessing. Beyond this, knowledge *of* God is transmissible through divine selection of individuals gifted with prophetic insight. Although Juadaic thought, as tradi-tionally interpreted, readily espouses the principle of divine revelation as on-going, its contemporary expression can employ insights derived from other faith communities regarding the nature of that inspired revelation.

Judaic thought appears to share with Taoism the idea of wholeness and completeness achievable through balance. Thus, it might be refreshed and strengthened in the pursuit of peace, harmony, and love of nature, as found particularly in the religious system of the Orient. This, of course, would require intensive cultural interchange.

Would that the Judaic faith had assimilated Hellenism more selectively into its corpus, particularly its aesthetic canons, such as the necessity for restraint in expressions of an art form. It may be appropriate to a literal religious fervor and ecstasy to shout explosively: "All my bones shall say, 'Who is like you, O God?'" (Psalms 35:2) Yet, the lack of restraint implicit in such ecstatic release is death to an art form. Thus, in contrast to the Hellenic ideal, Judaic thought has insisted on holiness as the paramount pursuit and, in its single-minded zeal that this ideal not be compromised, it tended to regard the pursuit of the purely aesthetic (even in its literary form) as a false god. (Incidentally, the early Puritans in England emulated this idea, regarding decorative art as idolatrous.) Hence, its music, in particular, has remained undernourished and threadbare, naive and child-like. While this may be a result of historical decentralization and rootlessness, it is also linked to the implications of the theological structure of the faith and its prescriptions: holiness – not the purely aesthetic – is beautiful. As Psalm 29:2 puts it: "Worship God in the *beauty* of holiness."

It should, of course, be pointed out that the history of the Jewish nation is one of fragmentation and splintering and that this has had no small effect on religious practices and beliefs. Some view this history as an actual good, as a preventive of a monolithic totalitarianism; yet, this seems to make a virtue of an historical odyssey. Surely, there is something to be said for a faith community that has an administrative machinery that promotes cohesive organization.

* * * * * * * * * *

A postscript may be added to the considerations here. Theological differences can produce violent conflict, as witness the history of the early Christian churches. Apart from that, there is yet a more important consideration. Much of the Christian and Jewish tradition, in particular, involved a bending of the knee in humility in the face of a *conception* of the divine. Yet, one may ask: to what purpose? The prophet Mikhah (Micah) suggested an answer some twenty-seven centuries ago.* The humbling of oneself is not for the purpose of securing favors from a grateful deity. Rather, it is to apprehend what loving kindness entails and in order to be able to *do* justice to fellow-humans. In the final analysis, what we *do* as an expression of our conceptions is more telling than the act of describing them.

*"Do justly, with loving kindnesses, walking in humility with God." (Micah 6:8)